Lasting Power of Attorney Made Simple

The Plain-English Beginner's Guide to Acting as an Attorney in England and Wales

Jim Steve Garner

This book is general information, not legal advice. It is written for people acting, or about to act, as an attorney under a Lasting Power of Attorney in England and Wales. Scotland and Northern Ireland have their own separate systems, which this book does not cover. Nothing here can replace advice from a solicitor who knows your specific situation, and reading it creates no solicitor and client relationship. The law and official guidance change over time. Where a decision carries real risk, or where large sums, property, disputes, or health choices are involved, please take proper professional advice.

The people and scenarios described in this book are composites, created to illustrate common situations that attorneys face. They are not real individuals. Any resemblance to actual persons, living or dead, or to actual events, is coincidental, and the names used represent no real person.

The author and publisher have made every effort to ensure the information was accurate at the time of writing. They accept no liability for any loss or damage caused, directly or indirectly, by acting or failing to act on anything contained in these pages. You remain responsible for your own decisions as an attorney and rely on this book at your own risk.

First edition, 2026

ISBN: 979-8-90599-283-4

Table of Contents

Preface

If you are holding this book, someone has trusted you with a great deal.

Maybe it is your mum, and her memory has started to slip. Maybe it is your dad after a stroke, a partner facing a long illness, or a friend who asked you years ago and has only now needed you to step in. Somewhere along the way, your name went onto a legal document, and now you are the person who pays the bills, talks to the bank, and makes the calls nobody wants to make.

You are not the first, and you are far from the only one. More than six million Lasting Powers of Attorney are now registered in England and Wales, with hundreds of thousands more added every year. Almost all of the attention goes on making one: the forms, the signatures, the registration. Far less is said about what happens next, when the document is actually used and an ordinary person becomes responsible for someone else's money, care, or home. That is where the real questions start, and it is exactly where most guidance goes quiet.

Here is the strange part. Nobody handed you an instruction manual.

You may have a thick registered document with an official stamp, full of words like "donor" and "severally" and "Office of the Public Guardian." You may have read the government website twice and still felt unsure what you are allowed to do on a normal Tuesday morning. You may lie awake worrying that one wrong move could land you in trouble, because you have heard, correctly, that an attorney can be held personally responsible for getting things wrong.

That worry is reasonable. It is also fixable.

It helps to be clear about what you are holding. A Lasting Power of Attorney is a legal document that lets one person, the donor, appoint another, the attorney, to make decisions for them. It comes in two forms, one for property and financial affairs and one for health and welfare. Being an attorney is not the same as setting the document up, and it is different again from deputyship, which a court grants when no valid power of attorney is in place. You do not own anything the donor owns. You hold the authority to act for them, within the limits set by the Mental Capacity Act 2005, and only in their interests.

Those limits are where good, honest people come unstuck. When does your authority actually begin? How do you prove it to a bank that keeps saying no? What records are you expected to keep, and for how long? The rules on gifts trip people up, and so do care fees, the family home, and the line between helping a relative and going too far. The official answers are out there, but they are scattered across pages written for administrators, not for the son or daughter sitting at the kitchen table with a folder of paperwork.

This book is the friend at that table who walks you through it. Not a solicitor talking over your head. Not a fifty-page factsheet that stops right where your real question starts. It follows the five principles of the Mental Capacity Act and puts them to work, one decision at a time, on the situations attorneys actually meet: the bank, the record keeping, the gifts, the care costs, the property, the health choices, the family fallout, and the enquiries from the Office of the Public Guardian. Each chapter teaches through short, real examples, then shows you what to do when the straightforward approach does not work.

You will learn what you can do, what you must do, and what you must never do. You will learn how to get the bank to take you seriously, and what records to keep so that nobody can accuse you of anything and make it stick. You will learn the gift rules that catch out good people, how to handle care costs and the family home, and what to do if a brother or sister starts making accusations.

A few honest words about scope. This is a plain-English guide, not legal advice, and it promises no particular outcome. It covers England and Wales, not Scotland or Northern Ireland, which run on different systems. The people and cases in these pages are composites, drawn to show common situations, and they describe no real person. Where a decision is genuinely big or genuinely stuck, the book will tell you plainly that it is time to get proper advice.

You do not need a law degree. You do not need to read this in order. Skip to the chapter that matches the fire you are fighting today, and come back to the rest when you can.

Let us get you steady.

Chapter 1.0: What You Just Became

Nicole opened the envelope at the kitchen table on a Sunday afternoon. Inside was a thick document with an official stamp from the Office of the Public Guardian. Her mother sat across from her, calm, a cup of tea going cold. "There," her mum said. "Now you can sort things out if I go doolally." They both laughed. Then her mum went to have a nap, and Nicole sat alone with the document, and the laughing stopped.

She had said yes to this two years ago without really understanding it. Back then it was a form. Now it was real. Her mum had been repeating herself, forgetting appointments, once leaving the gas on. The bank had started phoning Nicole about a payment her mum did not remember making. And here was this document that apparently made Nicole responsible for all of it.

She read the first page three times. She did not know what a "donor" was. She did not know if she could use this now or only later. She did not know if she was allowed to move money, pay the cleaner, or cancel the magazine subscriptions her mum no longer read. She googled it at eleven that night, closed nine tabs, and went to bed no wiser.

If you have had a version of that Sunday, you are in the right place. The document in your hands gives you real power and real responsibility, and almost nobody explains the difference between them. That is what this chapter fixes.

What you'll get from this chapter: By the end, you will know exactly what kind of attorney you are, what your document lets you do, and when you can start using it. You will understand the plain-English meaning of the words that keep tripping you up. Most of all, you will replace that vague, three-in-the-morning worry with a clear picture of the role you have stepped into. This is the foundation. Everything else in the book sits on top of it.

1.1 The Cast Of Characters

Before you can act, you need to know who is who. The document is full of formal words, and each one is simpler than it looks.

You are the **attorney**. That does not mean you are a lawyer. In this world, an attorney is just the person trusted to make decisions for someone else. That is you.

The person who trusted you is the **donor**. In Nicole's case, that is her mum. The donor is the one who made the Lasting Power of Attorney and chose you. It is their money, their home, their life. You are there to act for them, not instead of them.

The document itself is a **Lasting Power of Attorney**, which almost everyone shortens to **LPA**. It is a legal document that lets the donor appoint you to make decisions on their behalf if they cannot make those decisions themselves.

Sitting above all of this is the **Office of the Public Guardian**, known as the **OPG**. This is the government body that registers LPAs and keeps an eye on attorneys. Think of them as the referee. Most attorneys never hear from them. But they are there, and later chapters will show you how to stay firmly on their good side.

There is one more body worth naming now: the **Court of Protection**. This is a specialist court that steps in when something cannot be sorted out any other way. You will meet it properly in the final chapter. For now, just know it exists.

That is the whole cast. Donor, attorney, OPG, Court of Protection. Four terms, and you already know them.

1.2 The Two Different Jobs

Here is the part that confuses most people on day one. There is not one type of LPA. There are two, and they do completely different jobs.

The first is the **property and financial affairs LPA**. This one is about money. It lets you deal with the donor's bank accounts, pay their bills, manage their pension, deal with their savings, and, if it comes to it, sell their home. When people say "I've got power of attorney for Dad's money," this is what they mean.

The second is the **health and welfare LPA**. This one is about the person, not the pounds. It covers day-to-day care, where the donor lives, medical treatment, and similar decisions. It is a separate document and does a separate job.

A donor can make one, the other, or both. Your first task is to work out which one, or ones, you actually hold. Go and look. The type is printed clearly on the document.

Why does this matter so much? Because the two types switch on at different times, and mixing them up causes real trouble. Get this straight now and you will save yourself a great deal of confusion later.

1.3 When You Can Actually Start

People assume an LPA works like a light switch that only turns on when the donor "loses their mind." That is not quite right, and the truth is genuinely useful.

The **health and welfare LPA** can only be used once the donor is no longer able to make the particular decision themselves. While your mum can still decide where she lives and what treatment she wants, that decision stays hers. Full stop.

The **property and financial affairs LPA** is different. Once it is registered, it can be used straight away, but only with the donor's agreement, and only while they still have the ability to make those choices. That means you can help a donor who is physically frail but mentally sharp. You can go to the bank for them, pay bills for them, deal with paperwork they find tiring, all while they remain fully in charge and simply direct you.

This surprises people. A registered financial LPA does not mean the donor has lost anything. It is a tool the donor can switch on early to make their own life easier, with you as the willing pair of hands.

Here is the part most beginners miss. The ability to make decisions, which the law calls **mental capacity**, is not all or nothing, and it is not permanent. Your mum might be perfectly able to decide what to have for lunch and unable to understand a complicated investment on the same afternoon. Capacity is judged decision by decision, and it can change from day to day. You will meet this idea properly in the next chapter, because it sits at the heart of everything you do.

1.4 A Real Example

Meet David. His father, a retired bus driver, had a fall and then a slow decline. David held a registered property and financial affairs LPA and assumed it was useless until his dad "lost capacity" completely.

His dad was frail but sharp. He could not get to the bank, could not stand at the counter, could not manage the online banking his branch kept pushing. Bills started arriving in red. David kept thinking he had to wait for some official moment before he was allowed to step in.

David rang a helpline, half expecting to be told off for asking. Instead he learned that his registered financial LPA could be used right now, with his dad's blessing, precisely because his dad still had capacity. His dad did not have to lose anything for David to help. David simply became the pair of hands his father directed.

That afternoon they sat together. His dad told him which bills to pay and which direct debits to set up. David did the legwork. His dad stayed in charge of his own money, which mattered enormously to a proud man who had worked for fifty years.

What this means for you: A registered financial LPA is not a document you keep in a drawer until disaster strikes. Used with the donor's agreement while they still have capacity, it can make their life easier today. You do not have to wait for the worst.

1.5 The Things You Simply Cannot Do

An LPA gives you a lot of power. It does not give you all of it, and the limits are as important as the powers.

You cannot make or change the donor's will. A will is theirs alone, made while they have capacity, and no attorney can touch it.

You cannot treat the donor's money as your own. Their money stays their money, kept separate from yours, spent on them. This single rule prevents most of the trouble attorneys get into, and Chapter 5.0 shows you exactly how to honour it.

You cannot hand out the donor's money as large gifts. There are strict limits on gifts, and Chapter 6.0 is devoted to them because this is where honest people slip up.

If you hold a health and welfare LPA, you cannot refuse life-sustaining treatment on the donor's behalf unless the document specifically gives you that power. That box is either ticked or it is not. Chapter 9.0 covers this with the care it deserves.

And you can only make a decision for the donor once they are actually unable to make it themselves. You do not get to overrule a capable person just because you think you know better.

You might be thinking: this is a lot of rules, and I am going to get one wrong. That fear is normal, and it is the reason this book exists. The rules are learnable. You are already learning them.

1.6 A Second Real Example

Meet Priya. She and her brother were both named on their mother's financial LPA. Priya went to open a savings account so their mum's money could earn a better rate. The bank refused to give her a debit card or online access. She was baffled and, frankly, insulted.

The problem was not Priya. It was a single choice made two years earlier. When their mum set up the LPA, she had appointed Priya and her brother to act **jointly**, which means they must agree on and sign off every single decision together. That is different from acting **jointly and severally**, which would let either of them act alone.

A debit card is a single-user tool. A bank cannot issue one to two people who must act together on everything. Neither can it easily give online banking to a joint pair. The tick-box that felt like a small detail at the solicitor's office was now shaping everything Priya could and could not do.

Priya's mum still had capacity, so there was a route through. They could ask her to make a fresh LPA appointing them jointly and severally instead. It meant time and a new registration, but it unlocked the day-to-day banking they needed.

What this means for you: Before you do anything else, find out how you were appointed. Jointly, or jointly and severally, or jointly for some decisions and severally for others. This one fact quietly controls what banks will let you do, and if it needs changing, the time to change it is while the donor still has capacity.

1.7 When It Doesn't Work

The most common way this chapter falls apart is that you read your document, and it still does not make sense. The language is dense, the layout is odd, and you cannot tell if you hold one LPA or two, or how you were appointed.

This is not a you problem. These documents were designed by committee to be legally watertight, not friendly. Plenty of solicitors find them fiddly. Feeling lost reading one is the normal starting point, not a sign you are out of your depth.

Three things to try:

1. Find the front section where the type is named. Look for the words "property and financial affairs" or "health and welfare." Write down which one, or both, you hold on a sticky note and put it on the front.
2. Find the section on how the attorneys act. Look for "jointly" or "jointly and severally." If there is only one attorney

named, this does not apply to you and you can relax about it.

3. If you still cannot tell, ring the Office of the Public Guardian on their public helpline. They can confirm what is registered without charging you a penny, and they are used to exactly this question.

If it still will not come clear today, put it down. Come back tomorrow with fresh eyes. There is no deadline on understanding your own document, and it will still be there in the morning.

1.8 The Quick Version

You are the attorney. The person who trusted you is the donor. The document is the LPA, registered and watched over by the Office of the Public Guardian.

There are two types of LPA. The property and financial affairs LPA handles money and can be used as soon as it is registered, with the donor's agreement, while they still have capacity. The health and welfare LPA handles care and treatment and can only be used once the donor cannot make the particular decision themselves.

Your powers have hard limits. You cannot change a will, cannot treat the donor's money as your own, cannot make large gifts, and cannot refuse life-sustaining treatment unless the document specifically allows it.

Capacity is decided one decision at a time and can change from day to day. Finally, if there is more than one attorney, how you were appointed, jointly or jointly and severally, quietly shapes what you can do, especially at the bank. Go and check your document for those two facts today. They are the ground you will build on.

Chapter 2.0: The Five Rules You Follow

Marcus thought he was doing the kind thing. His mother had always been careful with money, and now that he held her financial LPA, he decided to protect her from herself. She wanted to give fifty pounds to a neighbour who had driven her to hospital. Marcus said no. She wanted to keep her own debit card in her purse "just in case." Marcus took it, quietly, and told himself it was for the best. She wanted to stay in her cold, cluttered house. Marcus started viewing care homes without telling her.

He was not stealing. He was not cruel. He loved her. But he had made a basic mistake that catches out thousands of well-meaning attorneys. He had decided that holding the LPA meant he was now in charge of his mother, when the law says something almost opposite.

A social worker visited, listened, and gently explained that Marcus had been getting it backwards. His mother still had capacity to make most of those choices. The LPA did not transfer her life to him. It appointed him to help, and to step in only for the specific decisions she genuinely could not make, and even then to make them her way, not his.

Marcus felt terrible. He had spent three months treating a capable adult like a child. But the fix was simple once he understood the five rules underneath it all. Those five rules are the spine of everything an attorney does, and once you know them, most hard situations answer themselves.

What you'll get from this chapter: You will learn the five principles of the Mental Capacity Act in plain English, without a single line of legal jargon left untranslated. You will understand what "acting in someone's best interests" actually means in practice, and why it is not the same as doing what you would want. You will finish with a simple test you can run on any decision, so that when a hard one lands, you already know how to think it through.

2.1 Where The Rules Come From

Every LPA in England and Wales exists because of one law, the **Mental Capacity Act 2005**, which most people shorten to the **MCA**. You do not need to read the Act. You need to know that it sets out five principles, and that these five are not friendly suggestions. They are legal requirements, and every decision you make as an attorney has to fit them.

Here they are, translated.

One. Assume the person can make their own decision unless it is shown they cannot. Start from "yes, they can," not "no, they can't."

Two. Help them decide before deciding for them. If a bit of support, a quieter room, a simpler explanation, or a better time of day would let them make the choice themselves, you owe them that first.

Three. People are allowed to make unwise decisions. A choice you think is daft does not prove someone lacks capacity. Capable adults get to be stubborn, sentimental, and wrong, same as you.

Four. If you do make a decision for them, it must be in their best interests. Not yours. Not the family's. Theirs.

Five. Choose the option that limits their freedom and rights the least. This is called the **least restrictive** option, and it means you always reach for the gentlest solution that actually works.

Read those five again. Marcus broke at least three of them before lunch on his first day.

2.2 Capacity Is Not All Or Nothing

The word **capacity** gets used as if a person either has it or has lost it, like car keys. That is not how the law sees it, and the real picture is far more useful to you.

Capacity means the ability to make a particular decision at a particular time. It is decision-specific. Your dad might lack the capacity to manage a share portfolio and keep every scrap of capacity to choose what he wears, who visits, and what he eats. Those are different decisions, and each gets judged on its own.

It is also time-specific. Capacity can come and go. Someone with dementia may be clear in the morning and muddled by evening. Someone recovering from a stroke or an infection may be unable to decide one week and perfectly able the next. An infection alone can cloud an older person's thinking and then lift entirely once treated.

So the honest question is never "has Mum lost capacity?" The honest question is "can Mum make this specific decision, right now, with the right support?" Sometimes the answer is yes, and then the decision is hers and you step back. Sometimes it is no, and then you step in, but only for that decision, and only for as long as she cannot make it.

This is the single idea that would have saved Marcus three months of grief.

2.3 What Best Interests Really Means

When the donor genuinely cannot make a decision, you make it for them, and it must be in their **best interests**. That phrase sounds obvious and is quietly one of the hardest parts of the job, because best interests does not mean what you would choose. It means what is right for them, seen through their eyes.

The Act gives you a checklist to work through, and it is worth keeping close. What did the donor want when they could tell you? What are their beliefs, their values, the things that always mattered to them? What would they say now if they could? Who else should you ask, family, carers, close friends who know them well? And can you wait, if the decision is not urgent, in case they regain the capacity to make it themselves?

Take a real example. Your mother spent forty years in the same village, loved her garden, hated a fuss, and always said she would rather manage than be waited on. A "best interests" decision about her care is not the one that is easiest for you or cheapest for the family. It is the one that honours the woman who loved that garden and hated a fuss.

You will not always get it perfectly right. Nobody does. What protects you is showing that you thought about it properly, in their terms, and wrote down your reasoning. That written note is worth more than a perfect outcome, and Chapter 5.0 shows you how to keep one without it taking over your life.

2.4 A Real Example

Meet Elena. Her father had advanced Parkinson's and could no longer manage his money, so Elena, holding his financial LPA, took over the bills. A harder question arrived when his beloved old car sat unused on the drive. Elena wanted to sell it. It was worth a few thousand pounds, and the money would help with his care.

Her instinct was pure logic. He cannot drive. The car is wasting away. Sell it. Done.

Then she stopped and ran it through the best interests checklist instead of her own convenience. Her father had rebuilt that car by hand in the 1980s. He still asked to sit in it on good days. Selling it was the sensible financial move and, for this particular man, possibly the wrong one. His comfort and his sense of himself were part of his interests too, not just his bank balance.

Elena did not force it. She waited, watched, and asked him on a clear morning what he wanted. He said, plainly, to keep it a while longer. So she kept it, wrote down why, and revisited the question months later when he had stopped asking about it. Then she sold it, gently, and recorded that reasoning too.

What this means for you: Best interests is bigger than money. The obvious, logical, efficient choice is sometimes not the right one for this specific person. Slow down, ask what mattered to them, and write down how you decided. That habit will protect you far more than always picking the "smart" option.

2.5 The Simple Decision Test

You cannot carry the whole Mental Capacity Act around in your head. You do not need to. For almost any decision, you can run a short test that keeps you inside the five rules.

First, ask: is this decision actually mine to make? Can the donor make it themselves right now, maybe with a little help? If yes, it is theirs. Support them and step back. You have just honoured rules one, two, and three.

Second, if the decision really is yours because they cannot make it, ask: what would they want? Picture the person they have always been. Consider what they told you, what they believed, what they valued. Ask others who know them. That is rule four, best interests.

Third, ask: is this the gentlest option that works? Is there a way to do this that takes less away from them, less control, less freedom, less of their independence? If there is, choose it. That is rule five, least restrictive.

Fourth, ask: could I explain this decision, calmly and clearly, to the Office of the Public Guardian in two years? If the answer makes you uneasy, that unease is information. Write down your reasoning now, while it is fresh.

Four questions. Mine to make? What would they want? Gentlest option? Could I explain it? Run any tricky decision through those, and you are acting like a careful attorney, which is exactly what the law asks of you.

2.6 A Second Real Example

Meet Hassan. His aunt, who had appointed him, developed dementia and became convinced that her long-dead husband was coming home and needed money for the journey. She wanted to withdraw two hundred pounds and leave it on the hall table for him.

Hassan's first instinct was to refuse flatly and explain that her husband had died. Every time he tried, she became distressed and accused Hassan of hiding the money. The mornings turned into arguments.

He thought about the five rules. Correcting her over and over was neither kind nor least restrictive, and it was not achieving anything except upset. The real interest here was her wellbeing, not winning the argument. He also had a duty to protect her from genuinely losing money.

So Hassan found a middle path. He did not hand over cash that would vanish, which protected her financially. But he stopped fighting the belief head-on. He sat with her, let her talk about her husband, and gently steered the day onwards. On her clearer days, she managed her small spending money herself, because on those days she had the capacity to. He wrote down what he was doing and why.

What this means for you: The five rules do not always point to a clean yes or no. Often they point to a wiser third option that protects the donor without stripping away their dignity or their remaining independence. Your job is to find that third option, not to win.

2.7 When It Doesn't Work

The most common failure here is the Marcus mistake. You start, with the best of intentions, to run the donor's whole life, because it feels safer and simpler than working out what they can still decide for themselves.

It goes wrong because it is the opposite of what the law asks. The Act starts from the person's freedom and lets you take over only the specific pieces they genuinely cannot manage. Taking more than that, even out of love, is both a breach of your duties and, usually, deeply upsetting for the donor.

Three things to try:

1. For one week, before every decision, ask only the first question: is this actually mine to make? You will be

surprised how often the honest answer is no, this is still theirs.

2. Give support before taking over. A slower conversation, a quiet room, a decision offered in the morning rather than the evening. See how much the donor can still do with a little help.
3. Write down the decisions you truly did have to make, with a line on why. Reading them back shows you whether you are stepping in only where needed, or quietly taking the whole wheel.

If you have been getting this backwards, do not spiral. Marcus got it wrong for three months and put it right. Noticing is the turn. Adjust from today.

2.8 What To Take Away

Every LPA runs on the Mental Capacity Act, which sets five rules you must follow. Assume capacity. Help the person decide first. Let them make unwise choices. Act in their best interests when a decision is truly yours. And always choose the least restrictive option.

Capacity is not all or nothing. It is judged one decision at a time, and it can change through the day and over the weeks. So the real question is never whether someone has "lost capacity," but whether they can make this particular decision, right now, with support.

Best interests means what is right for them, seen through their values and history, not what is easiest or most logical for you. When a decision is genuinely yours, run it through four questions. Is it mine to make? What would they want? Is this the gentlest option that works? Could I explain it in two years? Answer those honestly, write down your reasoning, and you are on solid ground.

Chapter 3.0: Proving The Paper

Aisha stood at the pharmacy counter holding her father's repeat prescription and a folder full of documents, and the assistant would not budge. "We need to see proof you can act for him," the assistant said. Aisha slid the LPA across. The assistant frowned at it, turned a few pages, and said she was not sure it counted and would have to ask the manager. The manager was on lunch. The queue behind Aisha grew. Her father sat in the car outside, waiting.

Aisha had done everything right. The LPA was genuine and registered. But she had brought the original, forty pages of it, and nobody at a pharmacy counter is trained to flick through forty pages and decide what is valid. She had also never made a single certified copy, so she could not simply hand over a clean, stamped version and leave the original safe at home.

She got the prescription eventually, after twenty minutes and a phone call. On the drive home she realised the problem would repeat itself everywhere. The bank, the utility company, the council, the GP, the pension provider. Each one would want proof, and each time she would be dragging the precious original into places it could easily be lost or damaged.

That evening she solved it once and for all, and the solution took an hour. The trick is not to fight this battle at every counter. The trick is to build a proof pack once, so that from then on, proving your authority is a two-minute job instead of a twenty-minute ordeal.

What you'll get from this chapter: You will learn what a registered LPA looks like and why registration matters. You will learn how to make certified copies so you never risk the original again. You will learn about the online service that lets organisations check the LPA in seconds, and what the coming digital changes mean for you. By the end you will have a proof pack ready to go, and the counter standoffs will mostly stop.

3.1 Registered Or Nothing

The first thing to understand is blunt. An LPA that has not been registered with the Office of the Public Guardian cannot be used at all. Not a little. Not in an emergency. Not at all.

Registration is the step that turns a signed form into a live legal power. When the OPG registers an LPA, they stamp it, and that stamp is what makes it real. Most people reading this book will already hold a registered LPA, so this is usually good news rather than a task. Go and look at your document. Somewhere near the front there will be an official stamp or a perforation from the OPG confirming registration and the date.

If you are looking at a signed LPA with no registration stamp, stop and sort that out before anything else, because you cannot act on it. And here is a point that catches families out badly. You can only make an LPA while the donor still has capacity. A validly made LPA can then be registered later, even after the donor has lost capacity, so an unregistered LPA that was properly made is not lost. The window that closes at capacity is the window to make an LPA in the first place. If the donor never made one before losing capacity, the family may be left applying to the Court of Protection instead, which is slower and far more expensive. If you are in that position, Chapter 12.0 explains the route.

For most of you, though, the document is registered, and the job now is simply proving it, over and over, to everyone who asks.

3.2 Make Copies Before You Need Them

Aisha's mistake was carrying the original everywhere. The fix is the **certified copy**.

A certified copy is a photocopy of the whole LPA that someone official has signed on every page to confirm it is a true copy of the original. Once you have certified copies, you can hand one to the bank, one to the pension provider, one to the council, and keep the original safe at home. If an organisation loses your copy, you shrug and send another. The original never leaves your care.

Who can certify a copy? The donor can, if they still have capacity. A solicitor or notary can, usually for a small fee. A chartered legal executive can. And there is a route where the donor certifies each page with a specific wording confirming it is a true and complete copy. If you are certifying copies, get the exact wording right, because a sloppily certified copy gets rejected, which defeats the point.

How many should you make? More than you think. Consider every organisation that touches the donor's money and care. Bank, building society, pension, utilities, council tax, GP, and any investments. Then make a few spares. Ten certified copies made in one sitting will save you months of small aggravations.

You might be thinking this sounds like effort you do not have time for. It is one hour that buys back ten. Do it early.

3.3 Proving It Online

There is now a faster way for many organisations to check an LPA, and it is worth knowing about because it can skip the paper entirely.

The OPG runs an online service, usually called "use a lasting power of attorney," which lets you generate a secure access code. You give that code to an organisation, they enter it on the OPG website, and they see a verified summary of the LPA straight from the source. No copies to certify, no originals to post, no forty pages for a counter assistant to squint at.

Not every organisation uses it yet, and older LPAs may need to be added to the system first, but where it works, it is the cleanest option going. When you contact a bank or provider, ask if they accept the OPG access code. If they do, your proof problem shrinks to reading out a code.

Keep the access details somewhere safe and private, the same way you would guard a password, because that code gives access to real authority. Treat it with the same care as the original document.

3.4 A Real Example

Meet James. His mother had savings spread across five different institutions, and he dreaded proving his authority to all of them. He pictured five trips, five queues, five arguments.

Instead he spent one evening building a proof pack. He had a solicitor certify eight copies of the LPA at a modest cost. He set up his mother's OPG access code and wrote the details in a locked note on his phone. He made a simple list of every institution, the account numbers, and a column to tick once each had accepted his authority.

Then he worked the list methodically. Two banks accepted the online access code and were done in a single phone call. Two took a certified copy by post. One, the awkward one, wanted him in a branch, and he brought a certified copy and left the original at home where it belonged.

Within two weeks, every institution had recorded him as attorney. He never once risked the original, and he still had spare certified copies in a drawer for the next organisation that asked.

What this means for you: Do the proving as a single project, not as a series of ambushes. A certified copy stack plus an online access code plus a checklist turns a dreaded ordeal into a fortnight of steady admin. Front-load the effort and the rest of the year gets easier.

3.5 What Is Changing

The system you are dealing with is in the middle of a shakeup, and it helps to know where things are heading so nothing surprises you.

The paper process for LPAs is decades old, and the government has passed the **Powers of Attorney Act 2023** to modernise it. The plan is to allow LPAs to be made and registered online, with identity checks built in, moving away from the slow shuffle of posted paper. This is being rolled out gradually, and a paper route is being kept for people who prefer it or cannot use the internet.

There is also a further Bill that has been working through Parliament aimed at making life easier for attorneys once the LPA is in use. Among its proposals are formal duties on banks and care homes to properly recognise and support a valid LPA, which, as the next chapter will show, cannot come soon enough for anyone who has been turned away at a counter.

None of this changes the core of your job. Register the LPA, prove it, act carefully, keep records. But it does mean the mechanics of proving an LPA will keep improving, and it is worth checking the official gov.uk pages now and then rather than relying on what a neighbour did five years ago.

3.6 Building Your Proof Pack Today

Here is how to turn this chapter into a finished task rather than a good intention.

Start by finding the registered original and confirming that stamp is there. Put the original somewhere safe and decide that it lives there, not in your handbag.

Next, get certified copies made. If the donor still has capacity and you are confident with the exact certifying wording, they can do it. If there is any doubt, pay a solicitor to certify a stack. It is money well spent for the peace of mind and the correct wording.

Then set up the OPG online access, if the LPA is on the system, and store the code as carefully as a bank password.

Finally, write a one-page list of every organisation that will need proof, with a tick-box for each. Work the list over a couple of weeks. Ask each one which they prefer, the online code or a certified copy, and give them what they want.

When the list is all ticked, you are done. Proof stops being a recurring fight and becomes a code you read out or a copy you post.

3.7 When It Doesn't Work

The most common snag is an organisation that rejects your certified copy or refuses the online code and insists on seeing the original in person. It feels obstructive, and sometimes it is, but there are ways through.

Why does it happen? Frontline staff are often nervous about LPAs and fall back on "bring the original" because it feels safest to them. It is rarely a real requirement, more a lack of training.

Three things to try:

1. Ask to speak to the organisation's specialist team. Banks and large providers usually have a dedicated power of attorney or vulnerable customer team who handle this all day and will not blink at a certified copy or an access code. The counter is the wrong place to fight this.
2. Offer the online access code as an alternative. Some staff do not know it exists. Naming it can unlock a faster route.
3. If they still insist on the original, take it in person, but never post it, and never leave it with them. Let them photocopy it in front of you and hand it straight back.

If one organisation is being impossible today, park it and move down your list. Momentum matters more than winning every skirmish on the same afternoon. Come back to the awkward one when you have the others behind you.

3.8 Wrapping Up

An LPA has to be registered with the Office of the Public Guardian before you can use it at all, and it can only be made while the donor still has capacity, though a validly made LPA can be registered later, even after capacity is lost. Most readers already hold a registered LPA. Check for the stamp and confirm it.

Do not carry the original into the world. Make certified copies, plenty of them, with the correct certifying wording, and keep the original safe at home. Set up the OPG online access code as well, because more and more organisations can verify an LPA in seconds using it.

Treat proving your authority as one focused project. A stack of certified copies, an access code guarded like a password, and a simple checklist of every organisation will carry you through in a fortnight. The system is being modernised under the Powers of Attorney Act 2023, and proving an LPA should keep getting easier, so check the official pages occasionally for the latest. Front-load the effort now and spare yourself a year of counter standoffs.

Chapter 4.0: Winning At The Bank

Lin took the morning off work, drove fifty miles to her aunt's branch because that was the only one that would see her, and arrived ten minutes early for her appointment. She waited seventy-five minutes past the appointment time. When she was finally seen, the clerk did not like her driving licence, questioned twenty-odd pieces of identification, and then, while Lin sat there, quietly phoned the aunt to ask security questions, telling the frail old woman that two people were in the bank trying to get into her account.

Lin was not a fraudster. She was a certified attorney trying to open a savings account so her aunt's money would earn a decent rate. She left in tears, having achieved nothing.

If you have a version of this story, you are not imagining it and you are not doing it wrong. The single most common and most maddening problem attorneys report is the bank. Not the law. Not the OPG. The bank. Branch staff who have never been trained on LPAs, processes that vary from one counter to the next, and outright refusals that seem to come from nowhere.

The good news is that this is a solvable problem, and it is solvable with preparation rather than luck. Lin went back a fortnight later, did three things differently, and walked out with the account open in twenty minutes. This chapter is those three things, and a few more besides.

What you'll get from this chapter: You will learn why banks make this so hard, and how to route around it. You will learn the appointment trap that silently blocks cards and online banking, and what to do about it. You will get a plan for the branch visit, and a clear escalation path for when a bank simply says no. By the end, the bank will be a task you can manage, not a wall you keep hitting.

4.1 Why Banks Are So Difficult

It helps to understand what you are up against, because it stops you taking it personally.

Frontline bank staff are trained, above all, to stop fraud and protect vulnerable customers. That is a good thing until it collides with a genuine attorney, at which point the very instincts that catch scammers start catching you. An LPA is unusual enough that many counter staff rarely see one, do not know their own bank's process, and default to caution. Caution, at a bank counter, looks like delay and refusal.

On top of that, processes vary wildly. One branch of a bank waves you through in ten minutes. Another branch of the same bank demands three forms of identification and a wait. The staff member who understands LPAs is off that day, and the one covering has never handled one. None of this is your fault, and none of it means your authority is in doubt.

There is help on the horizon. The reforms mentioned in the last chapter include proposals to place formal duties on banks to properly recognise and support valid LPAs. Until those bite, though, you win by being prepared, by going to the right people, and by knowing your escalation route. Let us get you there.

4.2 The Appointment Trap

Remember Priya from Chapter 1.0, refused a debit card because she and her brother were appointed jointly. This trap is common enough to deserve its own section, because it is the one banking problem that is not really the bank's fault.

If an LPA appoints two or more attorneys **jointly**, they must act together on everything. Every decision, every signature, both of them, always. A bank genuinely cannot issue a debit card in that situation, because a card is used by one person at a time, and that would breach the LPA. The same problem hits online banking, which also assumes a single user making a payment.

If the LPA appoints attorneys **jointly and severally**, any one of them can act alone. Banks can and do issue cards and online access on that basis, because a single attorney acting alone is exactly what the document allows.

So before you blame the bank, check your appointment type. If you are jointly appointed and this is crippling your day-to-day management, there is a route while the donor still has capacity. The donor can make a fresh LPA appointing you jointly and severally instead. It takes time and a new registration, but it fixes the problem at its source. If the donor has already lost capacity, you cannot change the appointment, and you may need to work within the limits or, in a real bind, ask the Court of Protection for help. Chapter 12.0 covers that.

The lesson lands hardest here for anyone still setting up an LPA. Jointly and severally is almost always the more practical choice for money. That one tick-box shapes years of banking.

4.3 Go To The Right People

Lin's first visit failed partly because she fought this battle at the counter. The counter is the worst place to prove an LPA. The person there is often the least trained for it and the most rushed.

Almost every bank and building society has a specialist team for exactly this. It goes by different names, power of attorney team, bereavement and power of attorney, vulnerable customer support, but it exists, and it is staffed by people who process LPAs all day and will not panic at the sight of one. Your job is to reach them, not to win over a counter assistant who is out of their depth.

Phone the bank's dedicated power of attorney line before you go anywhere. Ask them exactly what they need, in what form, and whether they accept a certified copy or the OPG online access code. Get the name of the team and, if you can, a reference number. Then, if you must visit a branch, you arrive with the specialist team's instructions in hand, which quietly overrides a lot of counter improvisation.

This one change, going to the specialist team instead of the counter, solves more bank problems than anything else in this chapter. Use it first.

4.4 A Real Example

Meet Carlos. His mother banked with a high street bank he found impossible. His first branch visit ended with a clerk rejecting his certified copy and refusing his suggestion to send the papers to a specialist team. He went home furious and stuck.

Then he changed tactics. He looked up the bank's dedicated power of attorney phone line, not the general number, and called it. The specialist who answered dealt with LPAs constantly. She told him precisely what she needed, took the details of his mother's registered LPA, and set up a secure way for him to send a certified copy directly to her team, bypassing the branch entirely.

Three days later, Carlos was registered on the account as attorney. He got online access because his mother had appointed him severally. The branch that had blocked him for a week was cut out of the loop completely.

What changed was not persistence at the counter. It was aiming at the right target. The counter had no idea what to do. The specialist team did this in their sleep.

What this means for you: When a branch blocks you, stop pushing there. Find the bank's specialist power of attorney team and deal with them directly. They are trained, they are quicker, and they will not reject your paperwork out of nervousness. The counter is the problem. The specialist team is the answer.

4.5 Savings, Platforms, And The Rate Trap

There is a particular frustration worth naming, because it blindsides careful attorneys. You do everything right, then find that a good savings account simply will not take an attorney at all.

Some savings providers and online savings platforms flatly refuse to open or run accounts under a power of attorney. There is no dramatic reason. Their systems and processes are not set up for it, and they will not change for one customer. It feels like discrimination, and attorneys have argued exactly that, but the practical reality is that some doors are closed and arguing at them wastes your energy.

The workaround is to shop for providers that welcome attorneys rather than fighting the ones that do not. Several banks and building societies handle LPA accounts well, often through a paper application rather than a slick app. When you are chasing a better interest rate for the donor's savings, add one question to your research before you fall in love with a rate. Do they accept power of attorney accounts, and by what process? Ask it first, and you will not waste hours on an application that was never going to complete.

Getting a good return on the donor's savings is part of managing their money well. Just accept early that your shortlist of providers is a little shorter than everyone else's, and choose from the ones that will actually have you.

4.6 A Second Real Example

Meet Fatima. She held her father's financial LPA and wanted to set up online payees so she could pay his carers and bills from home. Her father's bank told her that, as an attorney, she could not use the app or add new payees without a physical card reader that generated a one-time code. She ordered the card reader through the website. It never arrived. She ordered another. Weeks passed.

Fatima was doing nothing wrong. She had hit a clunky, attorney-specific process that the bank had bolted on for security and then failed to deliver. Meanwhile the bills waited.

She solved it by escalating properly. She rang the specialist team, explained that two card readers had failed to arrive, and asked them to either send one by tracked post or set up the payees for her over the phone with identity checks. Faced with a clear account of the failure, they set up the essential payees directly and posted a reader that actually arrived. She noted the dates and names of everyone she spoke to, which turned a vague grievance into a concrete complaint the bank had to act on.

What this means for you: Attorney processes at banks are often more awkward than normal customer processes, and things genuinely go wrong. Keep a note of every call, every name, and every promised action with dates. That record is what turns "the bank is useless" into a complaint they must resolve.

4.7 When It Doesn't Work

Sometimes you do everything right, reach the specialist team, provide perfect paperwork, and the bank still refuses or drags on for weeks. At that point you stop persuading and start escalating formally.

Why does it reach this stage? Usually a mix of a mistake on their side and a process that has stalled. Politeness has a ceiling. Beyond it, you need the bank's formal machinery.

Three things to try:

1. Put in a formal complaint, in writing, using the bank's official complaints process. State plainly that you are a registered attorney, that you have provided valid proof, and what you need them to do. Keep a copy. A written complaint gets logged and tracked in a way a phone moan does not.
2. Give them a deadline and reference the next step. Banks have a set time to resolve complaints. Tell them that if it is not resolved, you will take it to the Financial Ombudsman Service, which handles disputes between customers and financial firms for free.
3. If they still fail you, refer the complaint to the Financial Ombudsman Service. It costs you nothing, and banks take it seriously because it costs them.

If the whole thing is exhausting you, it is fine to pause the fight with one difficult bank while you sort the easier institutions. You do not have to win every battle at once. Protect your energy and come back to the hard one with your complaint in writing.

4.8 Before You Move On

The bank is the most common obstacle you will face, and it is beatable with preparation rather than luck. Understand that frontline staff are trained to stop fraud, so their caution catches genuine attorneys too. Do not take it personally, and do not fight it at the counter.

Check your appointment type first. Jointly appointed attorneys cannot be given single-user cards or app access, and the fix, while the donor still has capacity, is a fresh LPA appointing you jointly and severally. Then go straight to the bank's specialist power of attorney team rather than the counter. That single move solves most problems. Ask every provider up front whether they accept a certified copy or the OPG online code, and, for savings, whether they take attorney accounts at all before you chase a rate.

When a bank still fails you, escalate in writing through their complaints process, and take it to the Financial Ombudsman Service if needed. Keep a dated note of every call and name throughout, because that record is your power. Reforms are coming to make banks recognise LPAs properly, but until then, preparation wins.

Chapter 5.0: Records That Protect You

Two attorneys, same story, opposite endings.

The first, a man named Omar, kept a cheap notebook. Every time he spent his mother's money, he wrote the date, the amount, what it was for, and kept the receipt in a shoebox. It took him about two minutes a day and felt, honestly, like a waste of time. His mother had plenty of money and nobody was watching.

The second, a woman named Nicole, whom you met in Chapter 1.0, did not bother. She knew where the money went. It was obvious. Bills, shopping, the cleaner, the occasional treat. Why write down what she could plainly remember?

Two years later, a family member made a complaint to the Office of the Public Guardian about each of them. Not because either had done anything wrong. In both cases the complaint came from a relative who felt left out and suspicious. The OPG, as it must, asked each attorney to account for the money.

Omar opened his shoebox, handed over two years of dated notes and receipts, and the matter was closed within weeks. Nicole spent three months of evenings trying to reconstruct spending from bank statements, guessing at cash withdrawals, unable to prove what perfectly innocent payments had been for. She was cleared in the end, but it cost her a summer of stress she never needed to have.

The difference was not honesty. Both were honest. The difference was a notebook. This chapter is that notebook, and it is the cheapest insurance you will ever buy.

What you'll get from this chapter: You will learn exactly what records to keep, in what form, to a standard that satisfies the

OPG, and how to do it in a couple of minutes a day. You will learn the one rule about keeping money separate that prevents most attorney trouble. And you will get a simple everyday system for running the donor's regular bills and income without things slipping through the cracks.

5.1 The One Rule That Prevents Most Trouble

Before any notebook, there is a single rule that underpins everything. Keep the donor's money separate from your own. Always.

Their money lives in their accounts. Your money lives in yours. The two never blend. You do not pay the donor's bills from your account "to sort out later." You do not pop their cash into your wallet alongside your own. You do not let their money and yours share a pot even briefly.

Why does this matter so much? Because the moment money is mixed, it becomes impossible to prove whose was whose, and impossibility looks, to a suspicious eye, exactly like wrongdoing. An attorney who keeps funds cleanly separate can always show the truth. An attorney who has mixed them, even innocently, cannot, and ends up defending a mess of their own making.

The law is clear that an attorney must keep the donor's money and property separate from their own and keep accounts of how it is used. This is not bureaucratic fussiness. It is the wall that keeps you safe. Build it on day one and never let it crumble, not even for a single convenient transaction.

5.2 The Three Simple Records

Good record-keeping is not complicated. It comes down to three plain records, and you can run all three in a cheap notebook or a basic spreadsheet.

The first is a **running money record**, sometimes called a cash book. Every time money goes out of the donor's account, you write the date, the amount, and what it was for. Groceries, the gas bill, the window cleaner, forty pounds cash for the donor's own pocket money. That is it. A simple ledger of money out, with income noted too if you like.

The second is a **decision record**. This is for anything out of the ordinary, the non-routine choices. Deciding to move the donor into a care home, choosing to sell an asset, agreeing to pay a family member for care. For each, you write the date, the decision, and a few lines on why, tied back to the donor's best interests. You met this idea in Chapter 2.0. This is where it lives on paper.

The third is a **gift record**. Every gift you make from the donor's money, however small, goes here. The five pounds in a grandchild's birthday card, the flowers for a helpful neighbour. Chapter 6.0 explains the strict gift rules. For now, know that every single gift gets logged, no exceptions.

Three records. Money out, big decisions, and gifts. Keep receipts and statements to back them up, and you have built the shoebox that protected Omar.

5.3 Two Minutes A Day

You might be thinking this sounds like a part-time job you do not have time for. It is not. It is a habit that takes about as long as making a cup of tea, if you do it little and often instead of in a dreaded annual heap.

The trick is to record as you go. Paid a bill? Note it now, while you are already looking at the amount. Took cash out for the donor? Write it down before you forget what it was for. The whole thing collapses into an impossible chore only when you save it all up and try to reconstruct months later, which is precisely the trap Nicole fell into.

Pick a system you will actually use. A physical notebook by the kettle works beautifully for many people. A simple spreadsheet suits others. A dedicated folder for receipts, paper or photographed on your phone, catches the evidence. It does not matter which you choose. It matters that it is easy enough that you keep it up.

Here is the honest test. If your record-keeping is so fiddly that you dread it, you will stop, and stopping is the danger. Make it boring and quick. Boring and quick is what survives two years.

5.4 A Real Example

Meet Michael. He held his uncle's financial LPA and started out keeping no records, telling himself he would sort it out if anyone ever asked. His uncle had dementia and a suspicious son who lived abroad and resented Michael's involvement.

The son reported Michael to the OPG, alleging he was helping himself to the uncle's money. He was not. But when the OPG asked Michael to account for the past eighteen months, he had almost nothing. Statements, yes, but no explanation of the cash withdrawals, no receipts, no reasoning for the larger payments. Every innocent transaction now looked, on a bare statement, like it might be something.

Michael spent his evenings for three months rebuilding the picture. He phoned care agencies for old invoices, matched cash withdrawals to remembered shopping trips, and wrote long explanations of payments that would have taken one line to record at the time. He was eventually cleared. The OPG found no wrongdoing. But the ordeal was entirely self-inflicted.

The day it ended, he bought a notebook and started keeping the records he should have kept from the start.

What this means for you: A bare bank statement does not defend you. It shows money moving, not why. The explanation is the protection, and the explanation is almost impossible to reconstruct later and trivial to note at the time. Start the notebook today, not on the day a letter arrives.

5.5 Running The Everyday Money

Beyond the records, there is the ordinary work of keeping the donor's finances ticking over, and a little organisation stops things falling through the cracks.

Start by mapping the money on a single page. List the donor's regular income, their pension, any benefits, savings interest. Then list the regular outgoings, rent or mortgage, council tax, utilities, insurance, care costs, subscriptions. Seeing it all on one page tells you at a glance if the money coming in covers the money going out, and it stops you missing a bill or paying one twice.

Set up direct debits and standing orders for the predictable bills so they run themselves and you are not chasing due dates. Deal with pensions and benefits, and be aware that some benefits are managed through a separate arrangement with the Department for Work and Pensions called an appointeeship, which can sit alongside your LPA. If the donor's benefits are involved, check how they are being handled so nothing lapses.

Keep an eye on savings and investments too, managing them sensibly rather than boldly. Your job is to look after the donor's money with reasonable care, not to gamble it chasing spectacular returns.

And if the donor still has capacity for money decisions, keep them involved. Ask, explain, let them direct where they can. It honours the rules from Chapter 2.0 and it heads off the "you went behind my back" resentment that fuels so many family complaints.

5.6 A Second Real Example

Meet Amara. Her mother's finances were a tangle, several accounts, a couple of forgotten subscriptions, a pension paid into one bank and bills coming out of another that kept running dry. Nothing was wrong exactly, but money moved in ways Amara could not see clearly, and a direct debit had already bounced.

Amara spent one Sunday mapping it all on a single sheet. Income here, outgoings there. Straight away she spotted the problem. The pension landed in an account that had no bills attached, while the bill-paying account slowly emptied. She moved the essential bills onto the account the pension fed, cancelled two dead subscriptions, and set the whole lot to run on direct debits.

After that, her monthly job shrank to a five-minute check that income still covered outgoings and nothing odd had appeared. The bounced payments stopped. Her mother's money, once a source of low-level dread, became something Amara could see and trust.

What this means for you: Before you manage the donor's money day to day, get it onto one page. A single map of income and outgoings reveals the leaks and the traps, turns a tangle into a system, and shrinks your ongoing effort to a quick monthly glance.

5.7 When It Doesn't Work

The most common failure is not starting, or starting well and then quietly letting it slide after a busy fortnight. You mean to keep the notebook. Then a hard week hits, you miss a few days, the gap feels too big to fill, and you abandon it.

This is a habit problem, not a character flaw. A record kept perfectly for a month and then dropped is worth far less than a slightly scruffy one kept for years. The perfectionism is the enemy here, not the busyness.

Three things to try:

1. Shrink the record to the bare minimum. Date, amount, what for. Do not build a beautiful spreadsheet you will resent. Boring and quick survives.
2. Attach it to something you already do. Keep the notebook by the kettle, or set a two-minute phone reminder for the same time each evening. Habits stick when they lean on existing ones.
3. If you have already let it lapse, do not try to reconstruct the whole gap. Draw a line, note roughly where things stand today, and simply start keeping it properly from now. A clean restart beats a guilty non-start.

If life is genuinely too much right now, keep at least the receipts and statements in one folder, even without notes. That raw evidence buys you time to add the explanations later. The folder is the floor. Do not go below it.

5.8 The Short Answer

Keep the donor's money completely separate from your own, always. This one wall prevents most of the trouble attorneys fall into, because mixed money cannot be untangled and untangleable looks like guilt.

Keep three simple records. A running note of money out, a record of non-routine decisions with your reasons, and a log of every gift however small. Back them with receipts and statements. Do it as you go, two minutes at a time, in whatever cheap notebook or basic spreadsheet you will actually keep. A bare bank statement does not defend you. The written reason does, and it is trivial to note now and nearly impossible to rebuild later.

Alongside the records, run the everyday money on a system. Map income and outgoings on one page, automate the predictable bills, watch the pension and benefits, and keep a capable donor involved. The attorney with a shoebox of dated notes sleeps easily. The one relying on memory spends a summer he never needed defending himself. Be the one with the shoebox.

Chapter 6.0: The Gift Trap

Zara meant well. Her mother had always been generous, slipping twenty-pound notes to the grandchildren, sponsoring every charity walk, giving to the church. Now that her mother had dementia and Zara held the financial LPA, Zara kept the tradition going. She sent five hundred pounds to each grandchild at Christmas, "because Mum would have." She donated a thousand pounds to her mother's church building fund. She lent her own struggling brother two thousand pounds from her mother's savings, sure her mum would have wanted to help.

None of it went into Zara's pocket. Every penny went to people her mother loved. Zara thought she was being a good daughter.

Then the OPG investigated, prompted by another relative, and Zara discovered that she had broken the rules repeatedly. Not because she was dishonest, but because she did not know that an attorney's power to give away the donor's money is tightly limited. The generous Christmas gifts were too large. The church donation was not a gift the law allowed her to make. The loan to her brother needed permission she never sought. Zara faced having to repay money personally.

This is the trap that catches more good, honest attorneys than almost anything else. Gifts feel warm and natural, and the rules around them feel counterintuitive and mean. But the rules exist to protect the donor, and knowing them protects you. This chapter draws the lines clearly, so you never end up where Zara did.

What you'll get from this chapter: You will learn exactly what gifts you can make freely, what needs official permission, and what you must never do. You will get a simple traffic-light way to sort any gift you are considering. And you will learn the route for making a larger gift properly, on the rare occasions it is genuinely right, without putting yourself at risk.

6.1 Why Gifts Are So Restricted

Start with the reason, because it makes the rules make sense. The donor's money is meant to be spent on the donor. That is the whole point of the role. Giving it away, even to lovely people for lovely reasons, reduces what is there for the donor's own care and comfort, possibly for years to come.

The law worries about two things in particular. First, that a generous attorney might give away money the donor will later need, perhaps for care that costs far more than anyone expected. Second, that "gifts" can be a cover for an attorney quietly enriching themselves or their family. Because the law cannot read your heart, it draws bright lines that apply to everyone, the saints and the schemers alike.

So the power to make gifts from the donor's money is deliberately narrow. Under the Mental Capacity Act, an attorney can make only limited gifts, and anything beyond that needs the permission of the Court of Protection. It does not matter how sure you are that the donor would approve. It does not matter that the money is going to family. The limits apply regardless of intent.

Understanding this from the start saves you from Zara's fate. Generosity with someone else's money, however kind, is not yours to give freely.

6.2 What You Can Give Freely

Here is the good news. You are not forbidden from all gift-giving. The law allows an attorney to make modest, reasonable gifts on customary occasions, and to give reasonably to charities the donor already supported, so long as it is affordable given the donor's overall situation.

"Customary occasions" means the ordinary moments when gifts are normal. Birthdays, Christmas, a wedding, a religious festival the family marks. On those occasions, a reasonable gift to someone connected to the donor, a child, a grandchild, a close friend, is allowed.

Two words do the heavy lifting. **Reasonable** and **affordable**. A modest birthday gift to a grandchild from a comfortable donor is reasonable. Emptying a meaningful slice of the donor's savings into the same grandchild's account is not, even at Christmas. What counts as reasonable scales with the donor's wealth and, above all, with their needs. If the donor may face large care costs, the room for gifts shrinks, because that money may be needed.

Charitable giving follows the same logic. If the donor regularly gave to a particular charity, you can usually continue modest donations in the same spirit. Starting large new donations the donor never made is a different matter, and drifts into territory that needs permission.

Whatever you give, log it. Every gift, in the gift record from Chapter 5.0, however small. That log is your proof that you stayed within the lines.

6.3 The Gift Traffic Light

You will not carry the exact rules in your head every time a birthday comes round. So use a simple traffic light instead, and it will keep you safe.

Green means go. A small, reasonable gift on a customary occasion to someone close to the donor, affordable given the donor's finances and likely needs. A modest birthday or Christmas gift to a grandchild. A continuation of the donor's usual small charity giving. Log it and proceed.

Amber means stop and check. The gift is larger than modest, or it is not really tied to a customary occasion, or the donor's care costs make you unsure it is affordable. Anything that makes you hesitate is amber. Do not proceed on a hunch. Look at the official OPG guidance on gifts, and if still unsure, treat it as red.

Red means do not do it without permission. Large gifts. Loans to family. Interest-free lending of the donor's money. Gifting property. Anything done to reduce the donor's assets on purpose. Giving away money for inheritance-tax planning. All of these need the Court of Protection's approval before you act, not after.

Run every gift through the light. Green, log and go. Amber, stop and check. Red, seek permission or leave it alone. Zara's Christmas gifts were amber shading to red. Her loan and her big donation were red. The traffic light would have stopped her at every one.

6.4 A Real Example

Meet Ravi. His father, for whom he was attorney, had always given each of his four grandchildren a hundred pounds at Christmas. That first December as attorney, Ravi wondered if he was even allowed to continue.

He checked the guidance. A hundred pounds each, on Christmas, from a father who had always done exactly this and whose finances comfortably allowed it, was squarely green. It was reasonable, it was customary, it was affordable, and it matched a long-standing pattern. Ravi made the gifts, wrote each one in the gift record with the date and the recipient, and slept fine.

The following year, one grandchild was getting married. The family hinted that a generous wedding gift from grandad's savings would be lovely, perhaps a few thousand pounds. This felt different, and Ravi trusted that feeling. A few thousand pounds was well beyond modest, and his father might yet need that money for care. This was amber at best, more likely red.

Rather than guess, Ravi kept the wedding gift modest and in line with what his father might reasonably have given, and he noted his reasoning. Nobody could later say he had drained his father's savings on the family's say-so.

What this means for you: The same recipient can be green one year and red the next, depending on the amount and the occasion. Judge each gift on its size, its timing, and the donor's needs, not on who is receiving it. When your instinct says a gift is too big, listen to it.

6.5 Making A Larger Gift Properly

Sometimes a larger gift really is right. Perhaps the donor is wealthy, has clearly expressed wishes, and there is a genuine reason, and you feel strongly that a bigger gift or some inheritance-tax planning would honour them. You are not forbidden from ever doing this. You are forbidden from doing it on your own say-so.

The proper route is the Court of Protection. You apply to the court, explain the gift you want to make and why it is in the donor's interests or in keeping with their wishes, and the court decides. If it agrees, you are covered completely, because a court has authorised the gift. If it refuses, you have been saved from a serious mistake.

Yes, this takes time and effort, and usually some cost. That is the price of doing a big gift safely. Compare it to the alternative, which is making a large gift without permission, being ordered to repay it personally, and possibly being removed as attorney. The court application is cheap by comparison.

So the rule is simple. Small and customary, you handle yourself. Large, unusual, or strategic, you ask the court first. Never talk yourself into a big gift on the grounds that you are certain the donor would agree. Your certainty is not the authority. The court is.

6.6 A Second Real Example

Meet Jennifer. Her aunt, whose attorney she was, had significant savings and had often said she wanted to help Jennifer's daughter buy a first flat one day. Now the aunt had lost capacity, the daughter had found a flat, and a gift of fifteen thousand pounds would make the deposit.

Jennifer wanted to make the gift. Her aunt had genuinely wished it. But fifteen thousand pounds was firmly red, a large gift far beyond anything customary, and Jennifer knew that acting alone would put her in serious trouble, however honourable her intentions.

So she did it properly. She applied to the Court of Protection, set out her aunt's expressed wishes, the aunt's comfortable finances, and the reason for the gift. It took months and some cost. The court considered it and approved a gift, satisfied it fitted the aunt's wishes and did not threaten her care.

Jennifer made the gift with the court's blessing, recorded everything, and was completely protected. Had she simply transferred the money because she "knew" her aunt wanted it, she could have faced repaying it herself and losing the role.

What this means for you: When a large gift is genuinely justified, the answer is not to do it quietly and hope. The answer is to ask the Court of Protection first. It is slower and it costs, but it turns a dangerous act into a safe one and protects you entirely.

6.7 When It Doesn't Work

The most common failure is family pressure. Relatives lean on you to be generous with the donor's money, framing your caution as meanness. "Mum would have wanted it." "Don't be tight with Dad's money." "It's going to us eventually anyway." The pressure is real and it is hard to resist, especially at emotional moments like weddings and Christmas.

This goes wrong because the family's feelings, however sincere, are not the legal test. You are the one who answers to the OPG, not them, and you are the one who may have to repay an improper gift, not them. Their certainty does not become your authority.

Three things to try:

1. Put the rule on the family, not on yourself. Explain that the law limits what an attorney can give, that you could be personally liable for breaking it, and that this is not your meanness but the actual rules. Blame the rulebook.
2. Offer the proper route for anything large. Tell the family that a bigger gift is not impossible, but it needs the Court of

Protection's approval, and you are willing to apply if the case is strong. That turns "no" into "yes, correctly."

3. Log your reasoning when you decline or scale down a gift. A dated note explaining why you kept a gift modest protects you and shows you acted carefully, not coldly.

If the pressure is relentless, it is fine to slow everything down. No gift has to be made today. Delay is not refusal, and it gives heat time to cool and you time to check the guidance properly.

6.8 Pulling It Together

The donor's money is for the donor, so an attorney's power to give it away is deliberately narrow. You can make modest, reasonable gifts on customary occasions like birthdays and Christmas, and continue the donor's usual small charitable giving, as long as it is affordable given their finances and likely care needs. Everything larger needs permission.

Use the traffic light on every gift. Green is small, customary, and affordable, so log it and go. Amber is anything that makes you hesitate, so stop and check the guidance. Red is large gifts, loans, gifting property, and tax planning, none of which you may do without the Court of Protection's approval first.

When a big gift is genuinely right, apply to the court rather than acting alone. It is slower and costs money, but it protects you completely, while acting on your own certainty can leave you repaying the money personally and losing the role. Above all, do not let family pressure move the lines. Blame the rulebook, offer the proper route, and log why you decided as you did.

Chapter 7.0: Paying Family And Care

Diego and his sister split the care of their mother between them. His sister, who lived nearest, did most of it, giving up shifts at work to cook, clean, drive to appointments, and sit with their mum through long afternoons. Diego, holding the financial LPA, thought it only fair to pay her something from their mother's money for all that work. Their mum had savings. His sister was losing income. It seemed obvious.

So Diego started paying his sister a monthly sum from their mother's account. No paperwork, no agreement written down, no rate anyone could point to, just a transfer that felt right. It went on for a year.

Then their estranged brother heard about it and exploded. He accused Diego and his sister of siphoning off their mother's money under cover of "care." He reported it to the OPG. Suddenly a fair arrangement between two devoted children looked, on paper, like two attorneys quietly paying themselves from a vulnerable woman's savings, with nothing to show it was genuine.

Diego was not a thief. His sister had earned every penny and more. But the way they had done it left them exposed, because paying family from the donor's money is one of the sharpest conflict-of-interest problems an attorney faces, and it has to be handled with care and paperwork, not just good intentions. This chapter shows you how to do it safely.

What you'll get from this chapter: You will learn why paying family and yourself is so risky, and how to do it without falling into Diego's trap. You will learn what makes a family care payment defensible, how to reimburse your own costs correctly, and when a payment needs sign-off from others. By the end, you will be able to pay for genuine care fairly and keep yourself completely in the clear.

7.1 The Conflict At The Heart Of It

Start by naming the problem honestly. When you pay a family member, or yourself, from the donor's money, you are on both sides of the transaction. You control the money and you, or someone close to you, receive it. That is what lawyers call a **conflict of interest**, and it is exactly the situation the OPG watches most closely.

This does not make such payments forbidden. Family often provides the best care, and it is entirely reasonable that genuine care should be paid for from the donor's money, the same as it would be if a stranger provided it. The problem is never the payment itself. The problem is that a payment from you to your own family looks identical, on a bare bank statement, to helping yourself.

So the whole task is to make the difference visible. To leave a trail that shows, plainly, that this was real care, at a fair rate, arranged openly, in the donor's interests. Diego's payments were all of those things in reality and none of them on paper, which is why he ended up defending himself.

Get the trail right and family care payments are safe. Skip the trail and even the fairest arrangement can be made to look ugly by anyone who wants to cause trouble.

7.2 What Makes A Payment Defensible

A family care payment stands up when four things are true and written down.

First, the care is real. Someone is genuinely doing substantial work, cooking, personal care, transport, supervision, the sort of thing you would otherwise pay an agency to do. Vague "keeping an eye on Mum" is not the same as hours of genuine caring.

Second, the rate is fair. The payment should be reasonable for the work, roughly in line with what a care agency would charge for similar hours, not plucked from the air and not inflated. A defensible rate is one you could justify to a stranger.

Third, it is arranged openly. Other close family know about it. Where there are co-attorneys, they agree to it. Nobody is being kept in the dark, because secrecy is what turns a fair arrangement into a scandal.

Fourth, it is in the donor's best interests. Being cared for by a trusted family member, paid fairly, is often exactly what the donor would have wanted and cheaper and kinder than an agency. Write down why it serves the donor, not just the family.

Put those four together in a short written care arrangement, note the payments in your records, and you have turned Diego's exposure into a defensible, documented, fair deal. The paperwork is not bureaucracy. It is the thing that protects the very people doing the caring.

7.3 Paying Yourself

Paying yourself is the sharpest version of this, and it needs the most care, because here you are unmistakably on both sides.

There are two different things you might pay yourself for, and it helps to keep them separate. The first is reimbursing your out-of-pocket costs, the petrol driving the donor to hospital, the stamps, the shopping you bought with your own money for them.

This is not really paying yourself. It is getting back money you laid out on the donor's behalf, and it is fine, as long as you keep the receipts and record it clearly.

The second is paying yourself for care work you provide, the same situation as paying your sister, only now the sister is you. This is allowed in principle if the same four tests are met, real care, fair rate, openly arranged, in the donor's interests, but the conflict is at its most intense, so the trail must be at its most careful. Where there are co-attorneys, get their agreement. Where you are the only attorney, be especially transparent with the wider family and consider getting advice before you start.

If ever you are unsure whether paying yourself is proper, that doubt is a signal to seek advice or ask the Court of Protection. It is far better to ask first than to pay yourself for a year and have to justify it after a complaint.

7.4 A Real Example

Meet Sofia. Her father needed daily care, and Sofia, his attorney, gave up two days a week of her own paid work to provide it. Money was tight for her, and her father had savings and would happily have paid a carer. Paying Sofia for the care she provided seemed fair to everyone.

Remembering Diego's story, Sofia did it properly. She wrote a short care agreement setting out what she did, how many hours, and an hourly rate she based on what a local care agency charged for similar work. She emailed the arrangement to her two brothers, who both agreed in writing that it was fair. She recorded each payment in her father's accounts and noted in her decision record why paying her, rather than an agency, was in her father's best interests, familiar face, better care, lower cost.

A year later there was a family wobble when a cousin questioned the payments. Sofia simply produced the written agreement, the brothers' agreement, the rate comparison, and the records. The question evaporated in an afternoon. There was nothing to find, and she could prove it.

What this means for you: The difference between Diego and Sofia was not honesty. Both were honest. It was the paperwork. A short written agreement, a fair and justified rate, sign-off from the other family, and clear records turn a risky payment into a bulletproof one. Do the paperwork before the payment, not after the complaint.

7.5 When Care Costs More Than Family

Sometimes the honest answer is that family cannot provide the care the donor needs, and you are arranging paid care from an agency or a care home. This is more straightforward, because you are paying an unconnected third party, so the conflict of interest largely disappears.

Even so, a few things keep you safe. Choose care that suits the donor's needs and finances, and record why you chose it, tying it back to their best interests as you learned in Chapter 2.0. Keep the invoices and note the payments. Check that the cost is sustainable against the donor's income and savings, because care can be expensive and last for years, and running the donor short helps nobody.

Where care costs are large and ongoing, this shades into the territory of the next chapter, care fees and the family home, because paying for years of care may mean drawing down savings or selling property. For now, the point is simpler. Paying a genuine third party for genuine care is part of your job and rarely controversial, as long as you record what you are paying and why.

The controversial payments are almost always the ones that flow to you or your family. Third-party care, documented sensibly, is the calm part of the picture.

7.6 A Second Real Example

Meet Kenji. His mother's needs outgrew what he and his siblings could manage, and he arranged a place in a care home costing a substantial monthly sum. He worried about spending so much of her money.

Kenji handled it the way the rules ask. He looked at several homes, chose one that met his mother's needs at a fair cost, and wrote down why, her comfort, the standard of care, the location near family. He kept the contract and invoices. He checked the numbers against her pension and savings and worked out how long her money would last, so there would be no nasty surprise. He kept his siblings informed throughout.

When the same estranged relative who had caused trouble before questioned "why so much money is going out," Kenji showed the care home contract, the comparison of options, and his notes. It was plainly a real cost for real care, chosen carefully. There was nothing to argue with.

What this means for you: Paying an agency or care home for genuine care is a normal part of the role and rarely gets you into trouble, provided you choose sensibly, record your reasons, keep the invoices, and check the cost is sustainable. The scrutiny falls on money going to family, not on honest third-party care.

7.7 When It Doesn't Work

The most common failure is starting payments to family, including yourself, without any of the paperwork, because among family it feels cold and unnecessary to write things down. Then a rift opens, someone gets suspicious, and there is nothing to show the arrangement was fair.

This goes wrong because families change. The relative who was fine with it last year is furious this year after some unrelated falling-out, and now they weaponise the payments. Without a written trail, you cannot prove what everyone once agreed, and memory is no defence to the OPG.

Three things to try:

1. Write it down now, even if the payments started long ago. Draft the care arrangement, note the rate and the reasoning, and record it going forward. A late trail is far better than none, and it protects you from here on.
2. Get agreement in writing from co-attorneys and, ideally, close family. A short email confirming everyone thinks the arrangement is fair is worth its weight in gold if a dispute erupts later.
3. If the payments to family are large or the family is already tense, get advice, or ask the Court of Protection to approve the arrangement. External sign-off ends the argument before it starts.

If all of this feels like too much and the payments are small, consider pausing them until you have the paperwork sorted. It is better to delay a fair payment than to make it in a way you cannot defend.

7.8 One More Look

Paying family, including yourself, from the donor's money sits on a conflict of interest, because you control the money and a person close to you receives it. That does not make it forbidden. Genuine care deserves fair pay. It makes the paperwork essential, because a fair family payment and helping yourself look identical on a bare statement.

Make family care payments defensible with four things. Real care, a fair rate roughly in line with agency costs, an open arrangement that co-attorneys and close family agree to, and a clear best-interests reason, all written down before the payments start. Reimbursing your own out-of-pocket costs is simpler, just keep receipts. Paying yourself for care work is the sharpest conflict, so be most careful and most transparent, and seek advice or the court's approval if you are unsure.

Paying an agency or care home for genuine care is normal and rarely controversial, as long as you choose sensibly, record your reasons, and check the cost is sustainable. The scrutiny falls on money going to family. Diego and Sofia were equally honest. Only Sofia could prove it. Be Sofia.

Chapter 8.0: The House And The Fees

Layla faced the decision every attorney dreads. Her mother had moved permanently into a care home, the fees were eating into her savings, and the family house sat empty. Selling it would fund years of good care. But Layla's uncle had a different idea. "Don't sell it," he urged. "Sign it over to you and your sister now. Get it out of your mum's name before the council takes it all for fees. That's what everyone does."

It sounded clever. It sounded like protecting the family. It was also, as Layla nearly discovered the hard way, a route into serious trouble.

Moving the donor's home out of their name to dodge care fees has a name in the rules. It is called **deprivation of assets**, and councils can see straight through it. They can assess the donor as if they still owned the house, so the fees still have to be paid but the asset is gone. And an attorney who deliberately gave away the donor's biggest asset to avoid care costs is not protecting the family. They are breaching their duties and inviting an investigation, with no time limit on how far back it can look.

Layla, thankfully, checked before she acted. She learned the difference between managing the donor's home and assets properly, which is a core part of her job, and stripping them away to dodge fees, which is a trap. This chapter draws that line clearly, because the sums involved are large and the pressure to "be clever" is strong.

What you'll get from this chapter: You will learn the basics of how care is paid for, so the whole area stops being a fog. You will learn how to sell or manage the family home properly when it is genuinely in the donor's interests. And you will learn exactly where the deprivation of assets line sits, so you never cross it, however persuasive the uncle at the family table.

8.1 How Care Gets Paid For

The area feels murky, so here is the plain shape of it. When someone needs care, whether at home or in a care home, the question of who pays is decided partly by how much money and property they have.

Broadly, a local council carries out a financial assessment, often called a means test, looking at the person's income, savings, and sometimes their property. Above a certain level of assets, the person is expected to pay for their own care, and is known as a **self-funder**. Below it, the council contributes, on a sliding scale. The exact thresholds change over time and vary in detail, so check the current figures on the official pages rather than relying on what a neighbour paid years ago.

The family home is treated in a particular way. It may be counted as an asset in some situations and disregarded in others, for example while a spouse or certain other relatives still live there. This is genuinely technical, and it is one of the areas where a short conversation with a specialist care-fees adviser or the council can save a great deal of confusion and money.

Your job as attorney is not to become an expert in all of this. It is to understand the shape, get the donor properly assessed, pay what is genuinely due, and not do anything to hide assets or dodge fees improperly. Manage the money honestly, and the system, clunky as it is, works as intended.

8.2 Selling The Home Properly

There is nothing wrong with selling the donor's home when it is genuinely in their interests. This is often exactly the right thing to do, and it is well within your powers as a property and financial affairs attorney.

When would selling be right? When the donor has moved permanently into care and the empty house is a cost and a worry, and the proceeds are needed to fund that care. When the house is unsuitable and the donor's needs would be better met by the money it releases. In those situations, selling is careful management of the donor's assets for the donor's benefit, which is your role.

Do it properly and you are on solid ground. Get the house valued fairly, sell it at a proper market price rather than cheaply to a family member, and put every penny of the proceeds into the donor's own account, kept separate from yours as always. Record the decision and your reasoning in the decision log from Chapter 5.0, tying it to the donor's best interests. Consult the donor if they still have capacity, and consult close family where sensible.

Notice the theme. Selling the home to fund the donor's care, at a fair price, with the money going to the donor, is proper. It is the opposite of deprivation, because the asset is being used for the donor, not hidden from the council.

8.3 The Deprivation Line

Here is the line, drawn as plainly as it can be.

On one side is proper management. You spend the donor's money and use the donor's assets for the donor's own needs and benefit. You pay for their care, their comfort, their home. The money leaves, but it leaves for them. This is your job, and no council or investigator objects to it.

On the other side is deprivation of assets. You deliberately reduce the donor's assets to avoid paying for care, or to qualify for benefits, or to preserve an inheritance. You sign the house over to the children. You give away savings as the fees loom. You move money out of the donor's name so the council cannot count it. The motive is to dodge, not to benefit the donor.

Councils are alert to this, and the rules give them teeth. If they decide assets were deliberately given away to avoid care fees, they can assess the donor as if those assets still existed, so the fees remain payable but the asset is gone. There is no fixed time limit on how far back they can look. And for you as attorney, deliberately depriving the donor of assets is a breach of duty that can trigger an OPG investigation and personal consequences.

The test is honest and simple. Are you using this money or asset for the donor, or to keep it from the council? If it is for the donor, proceed and record it. If it is to dodge fees, stop, whoever is urging you on.

8.4 A Real Example

Meet Amanda. Her father was self-funding his care home from savings, and the savings were shrinking. A well-meaning friend told her to gift her father's remaining forty thousand pounds to the grandchildren now, "before it all goes on fees."

Amanda felt the pull. It seemed a waste to watch the money drain into care costs when it could go to the family. But she remembered the deprivation rules and ran the honest test. The only reason to make that gift was to stop the money going on her father's care. That was deprivation, plain and simple, and doing it would breach her duties, could be unwound by the council, and might see her investigated.

So she did not do it. She kept paying for her father's care from his own money, as it was intended, and recorded her reasoning for declining the gift. When the savings dropped low enough, she engaged with the council for a proper means-tested assessment, which is exactly the system working as designed.

Her father's money went on her father's care. That was never a waste. It was the point of having saved it.

What this means for you: The urge to preserve the donor's money for the family by moving it out of reach is one of the strongest and most dangerous you will face. Run the honest test every time. If the only real reason for a transaction is to avoid care fees, it is deprivation, and no amount of family logic makes it safe.

8.5 A Second Real Example

Meet Miguel. His mother moved into permanent care, and her modest house stood empty, costing money in insurance and upkeep while her care fees mounted. Miguel, her attorney, decided to sell it.

He did it by the book. He got three valuations, put the house on the open market, and accepted a fair price from an unconnected buyer, resisting a cousin's suggestion to sell it cheaply "within the family." The full proceeds went straight into his mother's own account. He recorded the decision and why it served her, funding good care, ending the drain of an empty house, in his decision log. He kept his siblings informed.

Nobody could call this deprivation, because it was the opposite. The asset was turned into money and spent on his mother's care, at full value, transparently. When the council later assessed her finances, everything was clear and above board.

Miguel had managed his mother's biggest asset exactly as an attorney should.

What this means for you: Selling the donor's home is not something to fear when it is genuinely in their interests. Get fair valuations, sell at a proper price to an unconnected buyer, put the money in the donor's account, and record your reasoning. Done openly for the donor's benefit, it is sound management, not deprivation.

8.6 When It Doesn't Work

The most common failure here is not a mistake you make alone. It is caving to family pressure to "protect" the donor's assets by giving them away or transferring the house. The pressure often comes wrapped in confident certainty that "everyone does this" and that you are foolish not to.

This goes wrong because the confident relatives will not be the ones held responsible. You will. The council can unwind the transfer, the fees remain due, and the OPG can investigate you personally. The people who urged you on face none of that.

Three things to try:

1. Move the responsibility to the rules, not yourself. Tell the family that transferring assets to dodge fees is deprivation of assets, that the council can see through it and charge anyway, and that you, as attorney, would be breaching your legal duties. It is not your caution. It is the law.
2. Get independent advice on care fees. A specialist care-fees adviser or the council can explain honestly what is and is not allowed, and what the home really means for the assessment. Facts cool a heated family debate.

3. When a genuine question arises, such as how the home is treated while a relative still lives there, ask the council or a specialist rather than guessing. Some of these rules have real nuance, and getting a proper answer beats acting on family folklore.

If the pressure is overwhelming, remember you can always decline to act quickly. No asset transfer has to happen today. Slowing down is not weakness. It is often the single thing that keeps a good attorney out of serious trouble.

8.7 Closing The Loop

Care is paid for partly according to how much money and property the donor has, decided through a council means test, with self-funders above a threshold paying their own way and the council contributing below it. The family home is treated in particular, sometimes technical, ways. Your job is to understand the shape, get the donor properly assessed, pay what is genuinely due, and hide nothing.

Selling the donor's home is proper and often right when it is in their interests, funding care or releasing money they need. Do it openly, at a fair market price to an unconnected buyer, with the proceeds going into the donor's own account and your reasoning recorded. That is sound management, not deprivation.

Deprivation of assets is the opposite, deliberately reducing the donor's assets to dodge care fees, qualify for benefits, or preserve an inheritance. Councils can see through it, assess the donor as if the assets remained, and there is no time limit. For you it is a breach of duty. Run the honest test on every big move. If it is for the donor, proceed and record it. If it is to dodge fees, refuse, however persuasive the uncle at the table. When in doubt on the technical points, get proper advice.

Chapter 9.0: Health And Welfare Choices

Isabella got a phone call from the hospital about her father, and she froze. He had been admitted confused and unwell, and a nurse was asking her, as his health and welfare attorney, about his care and where he should go next. Isabella did not know what she was allowed to decide. Could she choose his treatment? Could she insist he come home? Could she refuse things on his behalf? She had held the health and welfare LPA for three years and never once used it, and now, on a Tuesday afternoon, it was suddenly real and she had no idea of its edges.

She said, honestly, that she was not sure what her role was, and the nurse, kindly, talked her through it. Over the next hour Isabella learned what her welfare LPA actually did. It let her be involved in decisions about her father's care and where he lived, once he could not make those decisions himself. It did not make her a doctor. It did not let her demand any treatment she fancied. And on the biggest question of all, life-sustaining treatment, her power depended entirely on a single box in the document, which she now needed to check.

The health and welfare LPA is the quieter of the two, often unused for years, and then it matters enormously at the hardest moments. This chapter walks you through it before you are standing in a hospital corridor, so that if that call comes, you already know your role.

What you'll get from this chapter: You will learn when the health and welfare LPA switches on, what it covers, and its limits. You will learn the special rule about life-sustaining treatment and why you must check your document now. And you will learn how to make welfare decisions the right way, working with professionals rather than against them.

9.1 When It Switches On

The first thing to hold onto is that the health and welfare LPA is different from the financial one in a way that matters. It can only be used once the donor is unable to make the particular decision themselves.

While your father can decide where he lives and what treatment he wants, those decisions are his, even if you disagree with them, and even though you hold the LPA. The document sits dormant. Only when he genuinely cannot make a specific care or treatment decision does your authority for that decision come alive.

This ties straight back to Chapter 2.0. Capacity is decision-specific and can change. Your father might be unable to make a complex decision about his long-term care while fully able to say he wants a cup of tea and would rather not have visitors today. The welfare LPA gives you authority only over the decisions he cannot make, and only while he cannot make them.

So your first question in any welfare situation is the same as always. Can the donor make this particular decision themselves, right now, with support? If yes, it is theirs, and the LPA stays in its drawer. If no, and it is a health or welfare decision, your authority applies. Isabella's father, admitted confused, could not decide his immediate care, so her role was live. On a clearer day, it might not have been.

9.2 What It Covers And What It Doesn't

The health and welfare LPA covers a real but bounded set of decisions. It lets you be the decision-maker, when the donor cannot decide, on things like their daily routine and care, the kind of support they receive, and where they live, including a move into a care home. It lets you be consulted and involved in decisions about their medical treatment.

What it does not do is turn you into a clinician. You cannot demand a particular treatment simply because you want it. Doctors still decide what treatment is clinically appropriate to offer, and you cannot force them to provide something they judge is not right. Your role on treatment is to represent the donor, to say what they would have wanted, to consent or not on their behalf within what is being offered, and to be part of the best interests decision, not to overrule medical judgement.

There is also a hard limit worth stating plainly. A welfare attorney cannot use the LPA to insist the donor is kept somewhere against a proper assessment, and cannot make certain decisions the law reserves, such as consenting to some specific treatments the Act sets apart. These are edge cases most attorneys never meet, but they are a reminder that the LPA is powerful, not unlimited.

For the everyday, though, the shape is clear. Care, support, and where the donor lives are squarely yours when they cannot decide. Treatment is a shared conversation where you speak for the donor. That is the bulk of the job.

9.3 The Life-Sustaining Treatment Rule

Now the part that matters most and confuses most. There is one category of decision, life-sustaining treatment, that a welfare attorney can only make if the LPA specifically grants that power.

When the donor made the LPA, they had to choose, in the document itself, whether to give their attorney authority over life-sustaining treatment or to keep that authority elsewhere. It is a specific option, either selected or not. If it was selected, you have authority to be the decision-maker on life-sustaining treatment, within a best interests framework. If it was not selected, you do not, and those decisions rest with the doctors, who must still act in the donor's best interests and consult you.

You need to know, before any crisis, which way your document goes. This is not something to discover in a hospital corridor at the worst moment of your life. Go to your health and welfare LPA today and find the section on life-sustaining treatment. Read which option was chosen. Then you know, in advance, whether that heaviest of decisions could fall to you or not.

Whatever it says, remember this is best interests territory of the most serious kind. If you ever hold this authority and face such a decision, you will not be alone. You will make it with the medical team, guided above all by what the donor themselves would have wanted, and you can and should ask for all the support available. This is a moment to lean on the professionals around you, not to carry alone.

9.4 A Real Example

Meet Wei. His mother had a health and welfare LPA naming him, and he had never looked closely at it. When she developed a serious illness, Wei suddenly needed to know his role, and he sat down and read the document properly for the first time.

He found the life-sustaining treatment section and saw that his mother had chosen not to give her attorney authority over those decisions. That surprised him at first, then made sense. His mother had wanted doctors to lead on the gravest medical calls, with Wei consulted about what she would have wanted, but not carrying the final decision himself.

Knowing this changed how Wei prepared. He did not expect to be the one deciding on life-sustaining treatment, so he focused on what was his role, being a strong voice for his mother's wishes, making sure the medical team understood who she was and what she valued, and making the care and comfort decisions that were his to make.

When the difficult time came, there was no confusion and no panic about his authority. He knew his lane. He spoke for his mother, the doctors led on the medical decisions the LPA had left with them, and everyone worked from the same understanding.

What this means for you: Do not wait for a crisis to learn what your welfare LPA says about life-sustaining treatment. Read it now. Knowing in advance whether that authority is yours removes a terrible uncertainty from an already painful moment and lets you focus on the role you actually have.

9.5 Making Welfare Decisions Well

When a welfare decision is genuinely yours, the way you make it is the same best interests approach from Chapter 2.0, applied to care and treatment.

Start from the donor. What did they want when they could tell you? What did they value, fear, hope for? A person who always said they wanted to stay in their own home as long as possible, or who dreaded a particular kind of care, has told you something you must weigh heavily. Their past wishes are not just sentiment. They are central to the decision.

Consult the people around them. The medical and care teams bring their expertise. Family and close friends bring their knowledge of the person. Best interests decisions are meant to be made with others, not in isolation, and a decision reached together is both better and far easier to defend.

Choose the least restrictive option that meets the need, the same principle as ever. If the donor's needs can be met at home with support rather than in a care home, and that is what they would have wanted, that gentler option deserves real weight.

And record it. Even in health and welfare, keep a note of the significant decisions and your reasoning, as in Chapter 5.0. Then, if anyone ever questions how you decided your mother's care, you can show that you did it thoughtfully, in her terms, with the professionals, choosing the gentlest path that worked.

9.6 A Second Real Example

Meet Ananya. Her father, living with advancing dementia, reached the point where he could no longer safely live alone, and Ananya, his welfare attorney, had to decide where he should live. He could not make the decision himself, so it was hers.

Her instinct, and her siblings' preference, was a care home that was well-reviewed and convenient for the family. But Ananya slowed down and worked through best interests properly. Her father had spent his life saying he never wanted to leave his neighbourhood, that his garden and his street were everything to him. A home across the city, however good, would cut him off from all of it.

So Ananya looked harder. She found a way, with a care package and a place at a smaller home in his own area, to keep him close to the streets he loved, even though it was less convenient for the family. She consulted his GP and the care team, discussed it with her siblings, and recorded why she had chosen his familiarity over the family's convenience.

Her father settled far better than anyone expected, in a place that still felt like home. And Ananya had a clear record showing she had chosen for him, not for herself.

What this means for you: Welfare decisions, like financial ones, must serve the donor's values, not the family's convenience. Consult the professionals, weigh what the donor always wanted, choose the gentlest option that works, and record your reasoning. The right choice for this person may not be the easiest one for you.

9.7 When It Doesn't Work

The most common difficulty is disagreement with the medical or care team. You believe one thing is right for the donor, the professionals lean another way, and you are not sure how hard you can or should push.

This is uncomfortable because the lines feel unclear. You have real authority over some decisions and only a voice on others, and in a tense moment it is hard to know which is which. It is rarely anyone acting in bad faith. It is usually two sides who both care, seeing it differently.

Three things to try:

1. Get clear on whose decision it actually is. If it is a care or residence decision the LPA gives you and the donor cannot make it, your authority applies, and you should say so

calmly. If it is a clinical treatment decision, you are a central voice for the donor's wishes but not the sole decider. Naming which kind of decision it is often unlocks the conversation.

2. Ask for a best interests meeting. Where there is genuine disagreement, professionals can convene a meeting to work it through together, with everyone's views on the table. Asking for one is reasonable and often resolves things.
3. If a serious disagreement cannot be resolved, the Court of Protection can decide. This is rare and a last resort, but for the gravest deadlocks it exists, and Chapter 12.0 explains the route.

If the situation is frightening and you feel out of your depth, that is a signal to ask for help, not to soldier on alone. Hospitals and care services have people whose job is to support families through exactly this. Lean on them.

9.8 Where You Are Now

The health and welfare LPA can only be used once the donor cannot make the particular decision themselves. Until then, care and treatment choices stay theirs. When it is live, it covers their daily care, the support they receive, and where they live, and it makes you a central voice, though not the clinician, in decisions about their treatment.

The critical thing to know in advance is the life-sustaining treatment rule. A welfare attorney can only make those decisions if the LPA specifically grants that power, chosen as an option when the document was made. Read your document today and find out which way it goes, so you are never learning it in a hospital corridor.

Make welfare decisions the same way you make financial ones, through best interests. Start from what the donor wanted and valued, consult the professionals and the family, choose the least restrictive option that works, and record your reasoning. When you disagree with the medical team, get clear on whose decision it is, ask for a best interests meeting, and know the Court of Protection exists for the rare deadlock. Above all, in the hardest moments, ask for the support around you. You are not meant to carry this alone.

Chapter 10.0: Families Who Fight

Raj and his sister were named together as their mother's attorneys, and for a year it worked. Then their mother's care got harder and more expensive, and the cracks showed. Raj wanted to bring in more paid care. His sister wanted to do more herself and spend less. Every decision became a standoff. Emails went unanswered, then turned sharp. Their mother's affairs stalled while the two of them dug in.

It got worse. Their brother, who was not an attorney and lived far away, started phoning both of them with accusations. He was sure money was being wasted, or worse. He threatened to "report the pair of you." What had been a family became three people braced against each other, with a vulnerable woman in the middle and her affairs frozen.

Here is the truth almost every experienced attorney learns. The law is rarely the hardest part of this role. The family is. Disagreements between co-attorneys, and accusations from relatives who are not attorneys, cause more grief, more stalled decisions, and more sleepless nights than the Mental Capacity Act ever will.

Raj and his sister found a way through, not by winning, but by changing how they worked together and how they handled their brother. This chapter is that way through, because you can be word-perfect on every rule in this book and still be sunk by a family at war.

What you'll get from this chapter: You will learn how to work with co-attorneys without deadlock, how to break a genuine disagreement, and what to do if a co-attorney is acting badly. You will learn how to handle accusing relatives who hold no LPA, and how transparency protects you from all of it. By the end, the human side of this role will feel less like a minefield.

10.1 Knowing How You Must Work Together

If you are not the only attorney, everything starts with knowing how your LPA requires you to act together, because it sets the rules of engagement. You met this in Chapter 1.0. It is worth its own look here.

If you are appointed **jointly**, you must agree on and act together on every decision. Neither of you can act alone. That means real cooperation is not optional, it is legally required, and a permanent disagreement can genuinely paralyse everything.

If you are appointed **jointly and severally**, either of you can act alone. This is far more flexible, but it brings its own risk, that one attorney acts without telling the other, and the two of you end up working at cross purposes or worse.

There is also a middle option, where the LPA says you act jointly for some decisions and jointly and severally for others. If you have this, read carefully which decisions need both of you.

Knowing your setup tells you what good teamwork has to look like. Jointly appointed attorneys must build genuine consensus, because they have no choice. Jointly and severally appointed attorneys must build genuine communication, because the freedom to act alone can quietly turn into chaos. Either way, the answer is the same underneath. Talk, agree where you can, and keep each other in the loop.

10.2 The Transparency Habit

The single best protection against family conflict, whether from co-attorneys or accusing relatives, is transparency. Openness does not just feel nice. It removes the fuel that fires burn on, which is suspicion.

Most family accusations grow in the dark. A relative who cannot see what is happening imagines the worst. A co-attorney kept out of the loop assumes they are being cut out. The remedy is to make what you are doing visible, so there is nothing to imagine.

In practice this is simple. Keep the good records from Chapter 5.0, so the money is always accounted for. Share regular, brief updates with your co-attorney and, where sensible, with close family. A short monthly note saying what has been spent and decided, and why, works wonders. Invite the interested relatives to see the records if they wish. Someone who is shown everything has very little left to accuse you of.

This is the "records that protect you" idea from Chapter 5.0 doing a second job. Good records defend you against the OPG. Shared openly, they also defend you against your own family, by dissolving the suspicion before it hardens into a complaint.

You might be thinking that a hostile relative does not deserve updates. Maybe not. But sending them anyway is not about what they deserve. It is about leaving them nothing to work with.

10.3 Breaking A Deadlock

Sometimes co-attorneys genuinely cannot agree, and if you are jointly appointed, that deadlock stops everything. You need a way to break it that does not break the family.

Start by separating the decision from the history. Often co-attorneys are not really arguing about the care package. They are arguing about who did more, who was closer to Mum, who moved away. Name that quietly, to yourself at least, and try to bring the conversation back to the single question in front of you and what is genuinely best for the donor.

Bring in a neutral third party where you can. A social worker, the donor's GP, or a care professional can give an outside view on what the donor actually needs, which shifts the argument from "my opinion against yours" to "what does the person who knows care say." Facts from outside the family carry a weight family opinions do not.

Go back to the donor's wishes as the tie-breaker. Not what you want, not what your co-attorney wants, but what the donor would have wanted. That is the legal test anyway, and it is also the fairest way to settle a stalemate.

If a serious deadlock truly cannot be resolved and it is harming the donor's affairs, the Court of Protection can step in and decide, or resolve how the attorneys should proceed. It is a last resort, covered in Chapter 12.0, but knowing it exists can itself unstick a negotiation, because neither side wants it to come to that.

10.4 A Real Example

Meet Nicole, whom you met in Chapter 1.0, now a year into acting alongside her cousin as joint attorneys for an aunt. They had reached a bitter impasse over selling the aunt's flat to fund care. Nicole wanted to sell. Her cousin refused, convinced the aunt would recover enough to return home. Nothing moved for months while the empty flat cost money.

They were jointly appointed, so neither could act without the other, and the standoff was total. The relationship soured. Then

Nicole, remembering that the real test was the aunt's best interests and not either of their opinions, suggested they ask the aunt's care team and GP for an honest view on whether she could ever realistically go home.

The professionals were clear and gentle. The aunt's condition meant a return home was not realistic, and the flat could not safely be kept for her. That outside verdict changed everything. Nicole's cousin was not being stubborn out of malice. He had been clinging to hope. Given a straight professional answer, he could let go. They agreed to sell, recorded the reasoning together, and salvaged both the aunt's finances and their own relationship.

What this means for you: When co-attorneys deadlock, do not try to win the argument between yourselves. Bring in a neutral professional voice and anchor the decision to the donor's genuine best interests. An outside answer can free a co-attorney who is stuck for reasons that have nothing to do with being difficult.

10.5 When A Co-Attorney Goes Wrong

Occasionally the problem is not disagreement but genuine misconduct. A co-attorney is helping themselves, hiding spending, excluding you, or acting against the donor's interests. This is serious, and you have duties of your own that you cannot ignore.

If you have real evidence that a co-attorney is abusing their position, you cannot simply look away to keep the peace. Your duty is to the donor, not to family harmony. Raise it directly first if it is safe and sensible to do so. Sometimes what looks like misconduct is a misunderstanding that a frank conversation clears up.

If it is real and does not stop, you can and should report your concerns to the Office of the Public Guardian. The OPG investigates exactly this kind of thing, and reporting a genuinely abusive co-attorney is not betrayal. It is doing your job. Keep your own records clean and separate throughout, so that whatever the other attorney has done, your conduct is beyond question.

This is hard, because the abuser is often a sibling or close relative, and reporting them tears at the family. But an attorney who knowingly lets a co-attorney abuse a vulnerable donor is failing the person who trusted them both. Chapter 11.0 explains how OPG investigations work, so you know what you would be setting in motion.

10.6 A Second Real Example

Meet Marcus, whom you met in Chapter 2.0, now sharing his mother's attorneyship with his brother. Marcus noticed money leaving his mother's account that he could not explain, and his brother, the other attorney, brushed off his questions and then stopped replying altogether.

Marcus did not want to believe it. But the unexplained withdrawals continued, and his brother's evasiveness deepened his worry. He tried a direct, calm conversation, giving his brother every chance to explain. His brother became angry and defensive and offered nothing.

With genuine evidence and no innocent explanation, Marcus faced a painful choice, protect his brother or protect his mother. He chose his mother. He reported his concerns to the OPG, providing his own clean records and the unexplained transactions. It was one of the hardest things he had done, and it fractured his relationship with his brother. But his mother's money was being taken, and he could not, as her attorney, let it continue.

The OPG investigated. Because Marcus had kept his own conduct spotless and separate, the inquiry focused where it belonged, on his brother, not on him.

What this means for you: If a co-attorney is genuinely abusing the donor, your duty is to the donor, not to family peace. Give them a fair chance to explain, but if it is real and continues, report it, and keep your own records clean so your conduct is never in doubt. Protecting the donor sometimes means an act that feels like betrayal but is actually loyalty to the person who trusted you.

10.7 When It Doesn't Work

The most common failure is a relative who is not an attorney but who accuses, interferes, and threatens, no matter what you do. You share updates, you keep clean records, and still they insist you are up to something. It is exhausting and it can feel relentless.

This happens because the accusations are often not really about the money. They are about old family wounds, feeling excluded, guilt at not helping, or grief looking for somewhere to land. You cannot fix those with a spreadsheet, because the spreadsheet was never the real problem.

Three things to try:

1. Keep offering transparency anyway, in writing. Share the records and the reasoning, calmly, even to a hostile relative. You are not doing it to win them over. You are building a documented history of your own openness that protects you completely if they ever complain formally.

2. Set a boundary on the behaviour, not the person. It is fine to say you will share information but will not accept abuse, and to keep contact brief and factual. You do not owe anyone endless arguments.
3. Remember that a complaint to the OPG from a hostile relative is survivable, and often quickly, if your records are good. Chapter 11.0 shows why. Knowing that can take the fear out of the threats, because the threat loses its power once you are ready for it.

If a relative's hostility is genuinely affecting your wellbeing, it is fine to step back from the relationship while continuing to do the role properly. You can protect the donor and keep clean records without absorbing endless abuse. Protecting yourself is allowed too.

10.8 The Main Ideas

The hardest part of being an attorney is usually the family, not the law. If you share the role, know how you must act together, jointly meaning genuine consensus is required, jointly and severally meaning genuine communication is essential, and build your teamwork accordingly.

Transparency is your great protection. Most family conflict grows in the dark, fed by suspicion, so make what you do visible. Keep clean records, share regular brief updates, and invite interested relatives to see the accounts. Someone shown everything has little left to accuse you of. When co-attorneys deadlock, do not fight to win. Bring in a neutral professional voice and anchor the decision to the donor's genuine best interests, with the Court of Protection as a last resort.

If a co-attorney is truly abusing their position, your duty is to the donor, not to family peace. Give them a fair chance, then report genuine abuse to the OPG and keep your own conduct spotless. And when a non-attorney relative accuses you no matter what, keep offering documented transparency, set boundaries on the behaviour, and take comfort that a complaint backed by good records is survivable. Protect the donor, protect your records, and protect yourself.

Chapter 11.0: When The Guardian Calls

The letter arrived on a grey Wednesday, and Amara, whom you met in Chapter 5.0, felt her stomach drop before she had even opened it. Office of the Public Guardian, it said across the top. Inside, in careful official language, it told her that a concern had been raised about her management of her mother's finances, and that the OPG was making enquiries. It asked her to provide an account of the money she had handled and to respond to specific questions.

Amara had done nothing wrong. She knew that. But her hands still shook. Being investigated by a government body feels like being accused of a crime, and for a moment she was sure this was the beginning of something terrible, that she would be branded a thief, that she might lose everything.

None of that was true, and this chapter exists to make sure you know it before any such letter lands on your mat. An OPG enquiry is not a verdict. A complaint is not a finding. Many concerns raised turn out to be unfounded, some of them made by relatives with an axe to grind. The OPG's job is to check, fairly, and if you have acted properly and kept your records, checking is exactly what clears you.

Amara replied, calmly and fully, sent in the very records this book urged her to keep, and the matter closed. This chapter shows you how to be ready, how to respond if the call comes, and why the honest attorney has far less to fear than that grey-Wednesday feeling suggests.

What you'll get from this chapter: You will learn what triggers an OPG investigation, so you can avoid the avoidable ones. You will learn what the OPG can and cannot do. And you will learn exactly how to respond to an enquiry in a way that resolves it, calmly, quickly, and without doing yourself any damage.

11.1 What Sets An Investigation Off

Investigations do not come from nowhere, and knowing the common triggers helps you both avoid trouble and understand a letter if it comes.

The most frequent trigger is a report from someone else. A family member, often one who is not an attorney and feels excluded, raises a concern. A neighbour, a carer, a social worker, or a bank notices something and reports it. Anyone can raise a concern with the OPG, and many investigations begin exactly this way. As Chapter 10.0 showed, some of these come from genuine worry and some from family grievance dressed up as worry.

Certain things reliably draw attention. Gifts that look too large, the trap from Chapter 6.0. Money moving to the attorney or their family without explanation, the risk from Chapter 7.0. Signs that the donor's money is being used for someone other than the donor. Assets disappearing in ways that look like the deprivation from Chapter 8.0. An attorney who cannot or will not account for the money when asked.

Notice something. Almost every trigger is either an actual breach this book has already warned you about, or an appearance of one that good records would dispel. That is not a coincidence. The habits in the earlier chapters are precisely the habits that keep you out of an investigation, or carry you safely through one.

11.2 A Complaint Is Not A Finding

Hold onto this, because it is the single most important thing to understand about the whole process. Being investigated does not mean you have done anything wrong.

The OPG receives many concerns. It has a duty to look into them, because that is how vulnerable people are protected from the minority of attorneys who genuinely abuse the role. But looking into a concern is not the same as concluding you are guilty. A large share of enquiries end with no wrongdoing found, because the concern was mistaken, exaggerated, or malicious.

The OPG will not usually tell you who raised the concern, and it does not need you to know. Do not spend your energy trying to work out which relative reported you, and above all do not go on the attack against a suspected complainant. That helps you not at all and can make you look worse. The OPG cares about one thing, which is whether the donor's affairs have been handled properly. Answer that, and the source of the complaint becomes irrelevant.

So when that grey-Wednesday feeling hits, breathe. An honest attorney with decent records is not facing disaster. They are facing an afternoon of admin and a fair check that will very likely clear them. The letter feels like an accusation. It is really a question.

11.3 What The OPG Can Do

It helps to know the OPG's actual powers, so the fear is proportionate to the reality rather than to your imagination.

The OPG can ask you to account for how you have managed the donor's money and to answer questions. It can send a Court of Protection visitor to see the donor and look into the situation. If it finds problems, it has a range of responses that scale with the seriousness. For minor issues it may simply give guidance or a warning about how to do things properly. Where money has been wrongly spent, it can require the attorney to put it right, including repaying money personally.

For serious cases, the OPG can apply to the Court of Protection to suspend or remove an attorney, ending their authority. And where there is evidence of theft or fraud, it can refer the matter to the police, because taking a vulnerable person's money can be a crime.

That range matters. Most attorneys who come to the OPG's attention are not criminals, and most outcomes are at the mild end, guidance, a warning, a correction. The severe outcomes, removal and police referral, are for genuine, serious abuse. If you have acted honestly and kept records, you are nowhere near that end of the scale, even if a letter has arrived.

Knowing the ladder of responses also tells you why good conduct matters so much. Almost every serious outcome traces back to something this book has warned against, taken far enough. Stay within the rules and the worst outcomes are simply not on your horizon.

11.4 A Real Example

Meet Omar, whom you met in Chapter 5.0, the man with the shoebox of dated notes. A relative, resentful that Omar rather than they had been chosen, reported him to the OPG, alleging he was mismanaging his mother's money.

The OPG letter asked Omar to account for two years of spending. Where a less organised attorney would have panicked, Omar simply opened his shoebox. He had every payment dated and described, receipts filed, larger decisions explained, and every small gift logged. He compiled it into a clear, complete account and sent it in, with calm answers to each of the OPG's questions. He did not rant about the relative who had reported him. He just answered the questions.

The OPG reviewed his account, found everything in order, and closed the enquiry. The whole thing took a few weeks and cost Omar some worry but no real damage. The relative's accusation, having no substance and meeting a wall of clean records, went nowhere.

What this means for you: The records this book keeps urging you to keep are exactly what turns an investigation from a threat into an afternoon of admin. Omar's shoebox did not just satisfy the OPG. It made a malicious complaint collapse. Keep the records, and if the call ever comes, you answer it with paperwork instead of panic.

11.5 How To Respond If It Happens

If an OPG enquiry lands on you, how you respond shapes how it goes. Here is the approach that serves honest attorneys well.

Do not panic, and do not ignore it. The letter is not a disaster, but it is real, and it has deadlines. Read it carefully, note exactly what is being asked and by when, and plan to respond fully and on time.

Respond completely and honestly. Provide the account and records requested. Answer every question directly. If you made an innocent mistake somewhere, say so plainly and explain it, rather than hiding it. The OPG deals with honest imperfection very differently from concealment, and an attorney who is open about a genuine slip is treated far more kindly than one who covers up.

Do not attack the complainant. As Chapter 11.2 said, the source is not the point, and going after them makes you look defensive and difficult. Stay focused on showing that the donor's affairs were handled properly.

Get help if the matter is serious. For a straightforward enquiry with good records, most attorneys can respond themselves. But if the allegations are serious, if large sums are in question, or if you are out of your depth, this is a moment to instruct a solicitor who specialises in this area. That is not an admission of guilt. It is sensible protection, and it is exactly what the earlier chapters meant when they said some moments call for proper advice.

11.6 A Second Real Example

Meet Priya, whom you met in Chapter 1.0. An enquiry reached her not from a malicious relative but from a genuine gap. In her first months as attorney, before she found her feet, she had made a couple of small gifts to grandchildren that were slightly larger than the rules allowed, and had not logged them well. A watchful relative flagged it.

Priya's instinct was to panic and to minimise. She resisted both. When the OPG asked, she responded fully and honestly. She acknowledged the two early gifts, explained she had made them before she understood the gift limits, showed that she had since learned the rules and kept proper records, and offered to put right anything the OPG considered improper.

The OPG saw an honest attorney who had made a small, early, genuine mistake, understood it, and corrected her practice. Rather than any serious sanction, the outcome was guidance on gifts and confirmation of how to proceed. Because Priya was open rather than evasive, a real if minor breach was handled gently.

What this means for you: If you have made a genuine mistake, honesty is your best friend in an investigation. The OPG distinguishes sharply between an honest attorney who erred and learned, and one who conceals. Own a real error, show you have corrected it, and offer to put it right. That path leads to guidance, not disaster.

11.7 When It Doesn't Work

The most common failure in an investigation is the attorney who cannot account for the money, not because they stole it, but because they never kept records. Their innocence is real and completely unprovable, and an unprovable defence is a weak one against a body whose job is to check.

This goes wrong because the OPG cannot see into your heart. It can only see what you can show it. An honest attorney with no records looks, on the evidence available, exactly like a dishonest one, and the process cannot tell them apart without documents.

Three things to try:

1. Reconstruct as much as you honestly can. Gather bank statements, contact care agencies and utility companies for old invoices, and rebuild the picture as fully as possible. It is far harder than keeping records was, but a partial reconstruction beats a blank.
2. Be honest about the gap. Tell the OPG plainly that your record-keeping was poor and that you are rebuilding what you can. Openness about a failing is treated far better than bluster or silence.
3. Get professional help sooner rather than later if the sums are significant. A solicitor who knows OPG work can help you

present what you have in the best and clearest way and deal with the process properly.

If you are reading this before any letter has come and you recognise yourself as the attorney without records, do not wait for a crisis. Go back to Chapter 5.0 today and start keeping records from now, and gather what evidence of past spending you still can. The best time to prepare for an investigation is long before one begins.

11.8 The Short Version

An OPG investigation feels like an accusation and is really a question. Most enquiries begin with a concern raised by someone else, often a relative, and a complaint is not a finding. A large share end with no wrongdoing found, because the concern was mistaken or malicious. The triggers are mostly the very breaches this book has warned about, or appearances of them that good records dispel.

The OPG can ask you to account, send a visitor, give guidance or a warning, require you to repay wrongly spent money, apply to the court to remove you, or, for genuine fraud, refer you to the police. That range scales with seriousness, and honest attorneys with records sit at the mild end. If an enquiry comes, do not panic and do not ignore it. Respond fully and honestly by the deadline, own any genuine mistake and offer to put it right, do not attack the complainant, and get a specialist solicitor if it is serious.

The attorney who cannot account for the money, even when innocent, is the one who struggles, because innocence without records is unprovable. So the real lesson points backwards, to Chapter 5.0. Keep the records, and the grey-Wednesday letter becomes an afternoon of admin rather than the start of a nightmare.

Chapter 12.0: When The Role Ends

Elena, whom you met in Chapter 2.0, sat with a cup of tea and a strange, hollow feeling. Her father had died the week before. Amid the grief and the funeral arrangements, a practical question surfaced that she did not know how to answer. She still had his LPA, still had access to his accounts, and there were bills to settle and money to move. Could she carry on using the LPA to sort it all out? It seemed the natural, helpful thing to do.

It was also, she discovered just in time, completely wrong. The moment her father died, the LPA ended. Not tapered off, not wound down. Ended, instantly and entirely. Using it after his death, even to pay his own bills, would have been acting without authority, a serious error, however well meant.

Every attorney role ends somehow. Usually it is the donor's death, as with Elena. Sometimes it is because the donor recovers capacity and no longer needs you. Sometimes an attorney resigns, or is removed. And sometimes, before the end, a situation arises that the LPA simply cannot handle, and the Court of Protection has to step in. This final chapter covers all of it, the powers beyond your LPA, and the ways the role draws to a close, so that you finish this book knowing not just how to do the job, but how to lay it down properly.

What you'll get from this chapter: You will learn when a situation is beyond your LPA and the Court of Protection is needed. You will learn how an attorney can resign or be removed. And you will learn exactly what happens when the donor dies, including the crucial fact that the LPA ends at once. Then this book will say its goodbye.

12.1 When The Court Is Needed

Your LPA is powerful, but it does not cover everything, and part of being a good attorney is recognising the moments that are beyond it. Those moments belong to the **Court of Protection**, the specialist court you first met in Chapter 1.0.

Several situations need the court rather than your own authority. Large gifts and any deliberate estate or inheritance-tax planning, as Chapter 6.0 explained, need the court's approval before you act. Making or changing a will for someone who lacks capacity is not something any attorney can do, but the court can make what is called a statutory will. Selling a jointly owned property can sometimes need the court's involvement. And a serious, unbreakable deadlock, between co-attorneys or with the medical team, can be brought to the court to decide, as Chapters 9.0 and 10.0 noted.

There is also the situation where there is no valid LPA at all. If a person loses capacity without ever having made an LPA, no family member automatically gains the power to manage their affairs. Instead someone must apply to the Court of Protection to be appointed a **deputy**, which is like a court-supervised version of an attorney. Deputyship is slower, more expensive, and more closely monitored than attorneyship, which is exactly why making an LPA in good time is such a gift to a family, and why, if you know people who have not made one, gently encouraging them to do so while they still can is worth doing.

The court sounds daunting, and applications take time and money. But it exists precisely for the decisions too big or too stuck for an attorney to handle alone, and using it is not a failure. It is the right tool for the right problem.

12.2 Stepping Down

An attorney is not chained to the role forever. There are proper ways for it to end from your side, and knowing them matters, because circumstances change.

You can resign. Perhaps your own health fails, or you move away, or the role becomes too much alongside the rest of your life. An attorney who can no longer act well is entitled to step down, and doing so responsibly is far better than struggling on badly. There is a formal process for resigning, which involves notifying the donor and the OPG properly, and you should follow it rather than simply stopping. If the donor still has capacity, resigning also gives them the chance to appoint someone else.

You can also be removed. If the donor still has capacity, they can revoke the LPA and end your authority whenever they choose, because it was always their power to give and to take back. If you are not acting properly, the OPG can apply to the Court of Protection to remove you, as Chapter 11.0 described. And an LPA can simply come to an end if there are no attorneys left able to act and no replacement was named.

The honest point here is that stepping down when you genuinely cannot do the role well is not letting the donor down. It is protecting them. An overwhelmed or unwell attorney serves no one. If you reach that point, use the proper process, hand over cleanly, and let someone better placed take up the role.

12.3 The Day The Donor Dies

This is the one every attorney needs to understand clearly and in advance, because it arrives at the worst possible time and the rule is absolute.

When the donor dies, the LPA ends immediately. Your authority as attorney stops at the moment of death, completely. From that instant you have no power to use the LPA for anything, not to access their accounts, not to pay their bills, not to move their money, not even to tidy up their affairs. It does not matter that the tasks are helpful and the money is theirs. The authority is simply gone.

What happens instead is that responsibility for the deceased person's affairs passes to the **executor** named in their will, or, if there is no will, to an administrator appointed under the rules that apply when someone dies without one. That person, through a process usually involving probate, deals with the estate, pays the debts, and distributes what remains. It is a different role, governed by different law, and it may or may not be you.

So on the day the donor dies, your job as attorney is to stop, not to continue. Notify the institutions that the donor has died and that the LPA has ended. Hand over to the executor. And be aware that reforms are being discussed that would place a clear duty on attorneys to notify the OPG when a donor dies, so the register can be kept accurate. Check the current guidance at the time, but the core rule will not change. Death ends the LPA at once.

12.4 A Real Example

Meet Isabella, whom you met in Chapter 9.0. When her father died, she was, like Elena, tempted to keep using his LPA to sort out the practical mess of bills and accounts, because she still had access and it seemed kind and efficient.

She checked first, and learned the rule. The LPA had ended the moment her father died. She stopped using it that day. She contacted his bank, the pension provider, and the utilities to tell them he had died and that her LPA authority had ended, and she began the separate process of dealing with his estate as the executor named in his will, which meant applying for probate rather than reaching for the old LPA.

It was more work than simply carrying on would have been. But carrying on would have meant acting without authority, exposing her to real trouble at an already unbearable time. By stopping, notifying everyone, and moving to her proper role as executor, Isabella did it correctly and protected herself while she grieved.

What this means for you: When the donor dies, put the LPA down at once, however tempting it is to keep helping with it. Notify the institutions, and move to the separate process of dealing with the estate, whether that is you as executor or someone else. The LPA is over the instant the donor dies. Continuing to use it is a serious mistake, not a kindness.

12.5 A Second Real Example

Meet David, whom you met in Chapter 1.0. His father did not die but, after treatment for an infection and a good recovery, regained much of the capacity he had lost. Suddenly David faced a question few attorneys expect. What do you do when the donor gets better?

David handled it gracefully. He recognised that his father, now able to make his own decisions again, did not need David stepping in, and that continuing to act as though nothing had changed would breach the very first principle from Chapter 2.0, the assumption of capacity. So David stepped back. He handed control of the day-to-day money back to his father, kept the LPA in place and registered in case it was needed again in future, and returned to being a son who helped when asked rather than an attorney who acted.

His father was grateful and, frankly, relieved to have his independence back. David had used the LPA when it was needed and let go of it when it was not, which is exactly how the role is meant to work.

What this means for you: The role does not only end in loss. Sometimes the donor recovers, and then the right thing is to step back and return control to them, keeping the LPA ready in case it is needed again. Using your authority only when the donor genuinely cannot decide, and releasing it when they can, is the whole role in miniature.

12.6 When It Doesn't Work

The most common failure at the end is continuing to use the LPA after the donor has died, out of a genuine wish to be helpful, without realising the authority has vanished. It is an easy and understandable mistake, made by decent people at the hardest moment.

It goes wrong because grief and practicality pull you toward carrying on, while the law has already switched your authority off. Nobody sends you a warning at the moment of death. The change is instant and invisible, and the tasks still sitting there make it feel natural to keep going.

Three things to try:

1. Learn the rule now, before you need it. The LPA ends the instant the donor dies. Knowing that in advance is what stops the mistake, because in the moment you will not be reading a book, you will be grieving.
2. When the donor dies, notify rather than act. Tell the banks, pension providers, and utilities that the donor has died and

the LPA has ended. Notifying is your job now. Using the LPA is not.

3. Find out who the executor is and move responsibility to them, whether that is you in a different role or someone else. If it is you, the estate is dealt with through probate, not through the old LPA. Get advice if the estate is at all complicated.

If the donor's death has left you overwhelmed and unsure what to do, that is normal, and it is fine to get help. A solicitor can guide you through dealing with the estate. You do not have to know all of this instinctively. You only have to know the one rule, stop using the LPA, and ask for help with the rest.

12.7 Laying It Down

Every attorney role ends, and ending it properly is the last part of doing it well. The Court of Protection handles what your LPA cannot, large gifts and tax planning, statutory wills, some property sales, serious deadlocks, and the appointment of a deputy where no LPA was ever made. Using the court is not failure. It is the right tool for the biggest problems.

You can resign through the proper process if you can no longer act well, and stepping down when you must is protecting the donor, not letting them down. The donor can revoke the LPA while they have capacity, and the OPG can apply to remove an attorney who acts improperly. And when the donor dies, the LPA ends at once, completely. Stop using it that day, notify the institutions, and hand over to the executor, who deals with the estate through a separate process. Sometimes, gladly, the role ends because the donor recovers, and then you step back and return control to them.

You have reached the end of this book, and you began it, perhaps, sitting alone with a document you did not understand, feeling the weight of a trust you were not sure how to carry. Look at what you know now. You know the five rules and what best interests really means. You know how to prove your authority and win at the bank. You know the records that protect you, the gift trap that catches good people, and how to pay for care safely. You know the deprivation line, the welfare decisions, the family battles, the OPG, and the ending. You are not the same person who opened this book.

You will still get things wrong sometimes. Everyone does. But you now know where the lines are, when to get proper advice, and how to keep yourself and the donor safe. Someone trusted you with a great deal. You are ready to be worthy of it. Go steadily, keep your records, ask for help at the hard moments, and take care of the person who chose you. That is the whole job, and you can do it.

References

Administration of Estates Act 1925, c. 23. (1925). https://www.legislation.gov.uk/ukpga/Geo5/15-16/23/contents

Age UK. (2023). *Managing someone else's money (Factsheet 78)*. Age UK. https://www.ageuk.org.uk/information-advice/money-legal/

Age UK. (2023). *Paying for care and support at home (Factsheet 6)*. Age UK. https://www.ageuk.org.uk/information-advice/care/paying-for-care/

Age UK. (2023). *Powers of attorney (Factsheet 22)*. Age UK. https://www.ageuk.org.uk/information-advice/money-legal/legal-issues/powers-of-attorney/

Alzheimer's Society. (2023). *Family disagreements about care and money*. https://www.alzheimers.org.uk/get-support/

Alzheimer's Society. (2023). *Lasting power of attorney*. https://www.alzheimers.org.uk/get-support/legal-financial/lasting-power-of-attorney

Blake Morgan. (2025). *The modernisation of lasting powers of attorney*. https://www.blakemorgan.co.uk/the-modernisation-of-lasting-powers-of-attorney-significant-milestone-as-government-makes-decision-making-digital/

British Bankers' Association. (2017). *A guide for people wanting to manage a bank account for someone else*. UK Finance. https://www.ukfinance.org.uk/

British Medical Association. (2022). *Best interests decision-making for adults who lack capacity*.

https://www.bma.org.uk/advice-and-support/ethics/adults-who-lack-capacity/

British Medical Association. (2022). *Mental Capacity Act toolkit*. https://www.bma.org.uk/advice-and-support/ethics/adults-who-lack-capacity/mental-capacity-act-toolkit

Care Act 2014, c. 23. (2014). https://www.legislation.gov.uk/ukpga/2014/23/contents

Carers UK. (2023). *Paying a family member to provide care*. https://www.carersuk.org/help-and-advice/

Citizens Advice. (2023). *Managing affairs for someone else*. https://www.citizensadvice.org.uk/family/looking-after-people/managing-affairs-for-someone-else/

Compassion in Dying. (2023). *Health and welfare lasting power of attorney*. https://compassionindying.org.uk/

Court of Protection. (2024). *Apply to the Court of Protection*. GOV.UK. https://www.gov.uk/court-of-protection

Department for Constitutional Affairs. (2007). *Mental Capacity Act 2005: Code of Practice*. The Stationery Office. https://www.gov.uk/government/publications/mental-capacity-act-code-of-practice

Department of Health and Social Care. (2023). *Care and support statutory guidance: Deprivation of assets*. GOV.UK. https://www.gov.uk/government/publications/care-act-statutory-guidance

Financial Ombudsman Service. (2024). *Power of attorney and third-party access complaints*. https://www.financial-ombudsman.org.uk/consumers

GOV.UK. (2024). *Applying for probate*. https://www.gov.uk/applying-for-probate

GOV.UK. (2024). *Become a deputy for someone who lacks mental capacity*. https://www.gov.uk/become-deputy

GOV.UK. (2024). *Become an appointee for someone claiming benefits*. https://www.gov.uk/become-appointee-for-someone-claiming-benefits

GOV.UK. (2024). *End a lasting power of attorney*. https://www.gov.uk/power-of-attorney/end-permanently

GOV.UK. (2024). *Get help paying for social care*. https://www.gov.uk/paying-for-social-care

GOV.UK. (2024). *Health and welfare lasting power of attorney*. https://www.gov.uk/power-of-attorney/make-lasting-power-of-attorney

GOV.UK. (2024). *Make a lasting power of attorney: Certify a copy*. https://www.gov.uk/power-of-attorney/certify

GOV.UK. (2024). *Make decisions for someone: Mental capacity*. https://www.gov.uk/make-decisions-for-someone

GOV.UK. (2024). *Make, register or end a lasting power of attorney: Overview*. https://www.gov.uk/power-of-attorney

GOV.UK. (2024). *Manage someone's bank account: Power of attorney*. https://www.gov.uk/power-of-attorney/using-lasting-power-of-attorney

GOV.UK. (2024). *Office of the Public Guardian*. https://www.gov.uk/government/organisations/office-of-the-public-guardian

GOV.UK. (2024). *Register a lasting power of attorney*. https://www.gov.uk/power-of-attorney/register

GOV.UK. (2024). *Report a concern about an attorney, deputy or guardian*. https://www.gov.uk/report-concern-about-attorney-deputy-guardian

GOV.UK. (2024). *Use a lasting power of attorney*. https://www.gov.uk/use-lasting-power-of-attorney

Mental Capacity Act 2005, c. 9, s. 12. (2005). https://www.legislation.gov.uk/ukpga/2005/9/section/12

Mental Capacity Act 2005, c. 9. (2005). https://www.legislation.gov.uk/ukpga/2005/9/contents

Mind. (2023). *Lasting power of attorney and the Mental Capacity Act*. https://www.mind.org.uk/information-support/legal-rights/mental-capacity-act-2005/

Money Helper. (2023). *Paying for a care home and deprivation of assets*. https://www.moneyhelper.org.uk/

Money Saving Expert. (2024). *Power of attorney: Dealing with banks* [Community forum discussion]. https://forums.moneysavingexpert.com/

NHS. (2023). *Lasting power of attorney and mental capacity*. https://www.nhs.uk/conditions/social-care-and-support-guide/

Office of the Public Guardian. (2015). *Duties of an attorney under a lasting power of attorney*. GOV.UK. https://www.gov.uk/government/publications/lasting-power-of-attorney-duties

Office of the Public Guardian. (2019). *Giving gifts: A guide for those managing someone else's finances*. GOV.UK. https://www.gov.uk/government/publications/giving-gifts-a-guide-for-deputies-and-attorneys

Office of the Public Guardian. (2023). *A guide for people who want to make a lasting power of attorney*. GOV.UK. https://www.gov.uk/government/publications/make-a-lasting-power-of-attorney

Office of the Public Guardian. (2023). *How the Office of the Public Guardian investigates concerns*. GOV.UK. https://www.gov.uk/government/publications/how-the-office-of-the-public-guardian-investigates

Office of the Public Guardian. (2023). *Safeguarding policy*. GOV.UK. https://www.gov.uk/government/publications/safeguarding-policy-protecting-vulnerable-adults

Powers of Attorney Act 2023, c. 42. (2023). https://www.legislation.gov.uk/ukpga/2023/42/contents

Relate. (2023). *Managing family conflict over caring responsibilities*. https://www.relate.org.uk/

Social Care Institute for Excellence. (2022). *Direct payments and employing carers*. https://www.scie.org.uk/

Social Care Institute for Excellence. (2022). *Mental Capacity Act (MCA) resources*. https://www.scie.org.uk/mca/

Social Care Institute for Excellence. (2022). *The five principles of the Mental Capacity Act*. https://www.scie.org.uk/mca/introduction/mental-capacity-act-2005-at-a-glance

Society of Trust and Estate Practitioners. (2023). *Gifts by attorneys and deputies*. https://www.step.org/

The Law Society. (2024). *Find a solicitor: Powers of attorney and Court of Protection*. https://solicitors.lawsociety.org.uk/

The Law Society. (2024). *Powers of Attorney Act 2023*. https://www.lawsociety.org.uk/topics/private-client/powers-of-attorney-act

www.ingramcontent.com/pod-product-compliance
Lightning Source LLC
LaVergne TN
LVHW022109200926
848481LV00003B/1120
* 9 7 9 8 9 0 5 9 9 2 8 3 4 *